open
field

wooded
hillside

open
field

black willow windbreak

cabin

garden

pump
house

TOWN ROAD

apple
tree

black locust hillside

site for
first
cabin

hiking trail

open field

red pines

white
pine
windbreak

white pine stand

white pines

lupines

hiking trail

rairie

lupines

More Praise for Old Farm

A HISTORY

"To read *Old Farm* is to be the beneficiary of a labor of love. With his hands, Jerry Apps has stewarded his family's sixty-five acres of Wisconsin with care and commitment. With his words, Apps has honored that land by sharing its natural, cultural, and personal history. The result is an intimate portrait of one particular 'old farm' in Waushara County. In the spirit that imbues this story, however, Apps provides a universal demonstration of a land ethic at work."

CURT MEINE
Aldo Leopold Foundation
Author of *Aldo Leopold: His Life and Work*

"*Old Farm* neatly fits more of rural Wisconsin between its covers than a whole shelf full of books. Its message of honoring the land and passing it on in better condition to those who follow is more important today than ever."

BILL BERRY
Author of *Future of Farming and Rural Life in Wisconsin*

"My only fear is that Jerry Apps's heartfelt portrait of his Waushara County farm, woven from the many threads of its human and natural history and suffused with a rich sense of place, will draw attention to a part of Wisconsin that owes much of its charm to the inattention it's received."

TOM DAVIS
Former Senior Editor, *Wisconsin Trails* Magazine

"What Aldo Leopold did for Sand County, Jerry Apps has done for Roshara. Combined with Steve Apps's beautiful photography, *Old Farm: A History* is a loving portrait of place calling all of us to respect and value the land we live on, not only for ourselves, but also for all those who will follow us."

LaMOINE MacLAUGHLIN
Executive Director, Northern Lakes Center for the Arts, Amery, Wisconsin

A MIDWEST CONNECTIONS PICK
by the Midwest Booksellers Association

"What is a farm but a mute gospel?
The chaff and the wheat, weeds and plants, blight, rain, insects, sun—
it is a sacred emblem from the first furrow of spring to the last stack
which the snow of winter overtakes in the fields."

RALPH WALDO EMERSON

Old Farm

A HISTORY

Old Farm

A History

JERRY APPS

WITH PHOTOGRAPHS BY STEVE APPS

Wisconsin Historical Society Press

Published by the Wisconsin Historical Society Press
Publishers since 1855

© 2008 by the State Historical Society of Wisconsin

For permission to reuse material from *Old Farm: A History* (ISBN 978-0-87020-406-7), please access www.copyright.com or contact the Copyright Clearance Center, Inc. (CCC), 222 Rosewood Drive, Danvers, MA 01923, 978-750-8400. CCC is a not-for-profit organization that provides licenses and registration for a variety of users.

Photographs identified with WHi or WHS are from the Society's collections; address requests to reproduce these photos to the Visual Materials Archivist at Wisconsin Historical Society, 816 State Street, Madison, WI 53706.

wisconsin**history**.org

All photographs by Steve Apps unless otherwise credited.
Photographs on opening pages: page i, the prairie turns golden in fall; page ii, lupine; page iv, big bluestem

Printed in Canada

Designed by Steve Biel
Endsheet map by David Michael Miller

12 11 10 09 08   5 4 3 2 1

Library of Congress Cataloging-in-Publication Data

Apps, Jerold W., 1934–
  Old farm : a history / Jerry Apps ; with photographs by Steve Apps.
     p. cm.
  Includes bibliographical references and index.
  ISBN 978-0-87020-406-7 (hardcover : alk. paper) 1. Waushara County (Wis.)—History, Local.
2. Farm life—Wisconsin—Waushara County. 3. Apps, Jerold W., 1934— Homes and haunts—Wisconsin—Waushara County.
4. Waushara County (Wis.)—Biography. I. Apps, Steve. II. Title.
  F587.W35A77 2008
  977.5'5704—dc22
                        2008004316

∞ The paper used in this publication meets the minimum requirements of the American National Standard for Information Sciences—Permanence of Paper for Printed Library Materials, ANSI Z39.48-1992.

For Josh, Ben, Christian, Nicholas, and Elizabeth,
my grandchildren

Contents

Prairie grass in spring. Some of our grasses
grow three or more feet tall.

Acknowledgments

In 1967 I began writing a weekly column, "Outdoor Notebook," for the *Waushara Argus*. Publisher Howard Sanstadt, now deceased, suggested I include stories about my newly acquired farm. Howard both encouraged and instructed me over a period of ten years while I wrote 520 columns about happenings at my Waushara County property.

Professor Robert Gard, folklorist and writing instructor with the University of Wisconsin Extension, read several of my newspaper columns and suggested I write a book about my family's farm adventures. He helped me through the many challenges of book writing and became my writing mentor. To him I am ever grateful. *The Land Still Lives* was published by Wisconsin House in 1970. Brief excerpts appear in *Old Farm*.

Jim Christensen, Wisconsin Department of Natural Resources (DNR), became interested in our prairie restoration and our Karner blue butterfly population. He provided me with reference material, invited me to a Midwest conference on prairie restoration, and introduced me to Dave Lentz, also with the Wisconsin DNR. Dave is an expert on Karner blue butterflies, a nationally endangered species that needs lupines for its survival. Dave helped us first identify our Karner blues—we have several little blue butterflies that flit around our farm that are not Karner blues. He also read some of the manuscript and made important corrections.

Karner blue butterfly

Neil Dibold, Prairie Nursery, Westfield, Wisconsin, was of enormous help with the identification of wildflowers, grasses, and trees at our farm. I especially appreciate his help in not only correctly identifying the plants but providing accurate Latin names. My brother Darrel, a horticulture PhD, owns and operates a plant nursery in New Jersey. He was once part owner of my farm and helped me with plant identification and Latin names. My brother Donald, who owns thirty-five acres of the original farm and lives on the place, has been a constant source of information as we together recalled the years when we planted several thousand trees.

Pam Anderson, president of the Wild Rose Historical Society, helped me sort out Tom Stewart's Civil War military history. Several men named Tom Stewart fought in the Civil War, and I couldn't figure out which was the first owner of our farm. Pam pointed me in the right direction. Dorothy Luening, a volunteer with the Wisconsin Historical Society, helped me prepare a National Archives application to obtain detailed information about the correct Tom Stewart.

Marvin Wagner, then mayor of Wautoma, Wisconsin, and an active member of the Waushara County Historical Society, encouraged me in my historical diggings and gave me valuable information about Waushara County history.

Linda Steffen, head librarian at Patterson Memorial Library in Wild Rose, directed me toward the collection of *Wild Rose Times* newspapers, along with historical minutes of the Wild Rose village board that are shelved in the library. I used this material extensively.

Rob Nurre, Wisconsin Commissioner of Public Lands Office, was a font of information about early Wisconsin land surveys. He also helped me sort out the history of the Harrison monument used to mark survey section corners (I have one on my farm).

My son Steve, a photographer for the *Wisconsin State Journal*, took all the contemporary photos in the book. He also read and commented on the manuscript from its early development. My son Jeff, a businessman in Colorado, offers broad perspectives and gives me many useful comments on my various book projects, this one included. My daughter, Sue, an elementary teacher in Madison, has a keen editorial eye. She finds many errors that I miss, and she is always asking, "What is this? What does this mean?" It's helpful to have representatives from another generation ask questions about what I too often believe everyone knows.

My wife, Ruth, as she has for more than thirty-five years, reads every book manuscript, usually several times. I listen carefully to her suggestions for improving my writing and continue to thank her.

Kate Thompson, my Wisconsin Historical Society Press editor, constantly amazes me with her ability to take my sometimes poorly organized work and turn it into something much better than I thought possible. I can't thank her enough.

Introduction

This is a story of an old farm, a scant sixty-five acres in Waushara County, Wisconsin, about ninety miles north of Madison and forty-five miles west of Oshkosh. It is located in the Town of Rose, which was named by settlers who moved here from Rose, New York, in the mid-1800s.

The story is about the great glacier that slowly progressed from what is now Canada, digging out the valleys, forming the hills, and leaving behind stones of every shape and size when the ice retreated. It is about the Native Americans who lived on these acres for hundreds of years, tapping the maple trees, trapping the beaver and muskrat, and fishing the streams and lakes long before the first white explorers arrived.

The story is about the first settlers who tilled these hilly, sandy acres after breaking the ground with oxen and heavy-beamed breaking plows, turning under native grasses that sometimes grew taller than the ox teams.

And it is about the years that my family has owned these acres, from 1964 to the present. We've cared for this farm not so much to make a living as to enhance our lives.

From land that provided only a marginal living for its early owners, this place we call Roshara has provided much for my family and me. Each year we harvest the bounty of our garden; gather wild grapes, plums, and cherries for jelly; and cut a few trees for firewood to heat our cabin. We have undertaken one major logging operation to thin pine plantations and remove undesirable tree species. I have hunted deer here for more than four decades; more recently, I've hunted here with my brothers, sons, and nephews for turkeys, ducks, and grouse.

A grasshopper explores a daylily flower.

But far more significant than the material gifts are the spiritual ones we harvest from our farm during all the seasons of the year. More than anything, these sandy acres, some wooded, some prairie, and some wetland, have enhanced our lives and given us new, richer perspectives about the land and all that it comprises.

As we have taken from this farm and at the same time labored to preserve and protect it, we have struggled with age-old questions about people's relationship to the land. The natural world is a vast expanse of overlapping layers of facts, ideas, and perspectives, understandable at one level and incomprehensible at another. It is always the same, yet always changing. It is science and mystery, chaos and calm. Its value exceeds by many times the sum of its parts.

Botanists and zoologists, ecologists and environmentalists have long sought to label, categorize, research, and understand the elements of nature. But they are deluded in thinking that they understand, that they *know*, once they have labeled and categorized. Such work is only a feeble beginning in comprehending the natural world and its intricate relationships.

Likewise, much of our learning about the land is draped in technical matters: classification, scientific study, and cause-and-effect relationships. What is often missing is what Aldo Leopold called a land ethic. Story and history. Community and compassion. The bigger picture.

To value the land and the natural world demands an appreciation that goes deeper than knowing, deeper even than understanding—to the level that involves not only the head, but also the heart.

Built by John Coombes nearly one hundred years ago, the pump house is one of the original farm buildings.

PART I

Beginnings

Rabbit-foot clover

Chapter 1

◇◇◇◇◇◇◇◇◇◇◇◇◇◇◇◇◇◇

Our Farm

"One swallow does not make a summer, but one skein of geese,
cleaving the murk of a March thaw, is the spring."
ALDO LEOPOLD

I grew up with my brothers, twins Donald and Darrel, on a 160-acre farm in Waushara County, Wisconsin. My parents, Herman and Eleanor Apps, farmed through the Depression years of the 1930s, the war years of the early 1940s, and the postwar years when farming changed dramatically—tractors replaced horses, electricity replaced lamps and lanterns, milking machines took over from hand milking, grain combines made threshing crews obsolete, indoor plumbing became available, and television eliminated much neighborhood visiting.

After my brothers and I left the home farm in the 1950s, Dad continued farming by himself, caring for a small herd of Holstein cattle and raising enough crops to support the cows. In 1964 Dad sold his cows at auction, and we knew he would eventually sell the farm as well. We all understood that walking the fields of the home place would soon come to an end.

By the mid-1960s I was married and had three small children. We lived in Madison, where I taught agricultural education courses at the University of Wisconsin and Ruth taught part time at Madison Area Technical College, but we continued visiting the home farm regularly. I wanted my children, two sons and a daughter, to experience some of what I had experienced as a child, to gain the appreciation for the land that I had acquired by growing up on a farm. I longed to buy some land of my own, but supporting a family on teachers' salaries left no money for purchasing a place in the country.

The mid-1960s were difficult years in this country. After the Gulf of Tonkin Resolution on August 7, 1964, the United States began sending large numbers of troops to Vietnam. By the end of 1965 troop levels had increased to 125,000 and B-52 bombers began their bombing runs. Sit-ins and student protests against U.S. involvement sprung up on college campuses around the nation, starting at the University of Michigan at Ann Arbor on March 24, 1965. The University of Wisconsin's Madison campus became a center of protest, with sit-ins, police-student confrontations, confusion, demonstrations, and tear gas hanging heavy in the night air. Sirens blared; bullhorns blasted for attention.

The contrast between the UW–Madison campus and life in Waushara County at that time was nearly unfathomable. The home farm was a peaceful place. But as they tended their crops and milked their cows, farmers were well aware that several thousand miles away a war raged. Several local boys had been drafted. Newspaper headlines shouted about battles and deaths.

But the war and the protests weren't the only reason for my interest in returning to the country. As a boy growing up in rural Wisconsin, I had developed an abiding interest in forestry, wildflowers, wildlife, and the outdoors. One of my favorite 4-H Club projects was forestry: during the mid-1940s I planted a few hundred trees each year on the home farm and kept a careful record of their survival and growth rates. By the mid-1960s many of these trees were twenty feet tall.

Knowing my interest in nature and the out-of-doors, my high school speech teacher, Paul Wright, encouraged me to write an original oration for the state high school forensics competition. My speech, "The Hole in Uncle Sam's Pocket," called for soil conservation. I received a runner-up award at a regional speaking contest in Stevens Point.

In 1959, when I worked for the University of Wisconsin as a 4-H youth agent, I read Aldo Leopold's now-famous book *A Sand County Almanac*, published the year after Leopold's death in 1948. I discovered a copy while supervising a group at a 4-H conservation camp. I was amazed at Leopold's writing skills and his ability to talk about the land and its preservation in fresh ways.

From Leopold I learned that a relationship with the land involves much more than hiking and identifying, more than wood chopping and tree planting. I learned that a true connection to the land requires thinking, feeling, and acting that comes from deep within and that can be cultivated and nurtured throughout a lifetime.

Soon I was reading about another Wisconsin boy, John Muir, born in Scotland in 1838 but raised here in Marquette County. Muir has rightfully been called the father of our national park system. His wonderful little book *The Story of My Boyhood and Youth* set the stage for his career devoted to the study of nature and the protection of the environment. Muir taught me the power of wonder, of searching and exploring, of looking and, more important, learning how to see. He helped me recognize the importance of leaving something of value for the next generation—a little piece of the outdoors to enjoy and appreciate.

I first learned about Henry David Thoreau in high school but at the time had little love for his writing. As I grew older I appreciated his words more and more. Thoreau's writing has taken me some work to decipher, but its philosophical perspective and deep insights into the natural world continue to impress me. In *Walden*, he wrote, "I found in myself, and still find, an instinct toward a higher, or, as it is named, spiritual life, as do most men, and another toward a primitive rank and savage one, and I reverence them both. I love the wild not less than the good." Those words require some pondering, but that's what I like about his work. Every time I read Thoreau, I discover new meanings and ideas. And I admire Thoreau's simple lifestyle, his craving for solitude, and his vast curiosity about all things in the natural world.

My high school English teacher, Miss Arlene Holt, introduced me to Ralph Waldo Emerson, but not until maybe twenty years ago did I discover his powerful book *Nature*. There I encountered the stunning, "Nothing in nature is exhausted in its first use. When a thing has served an end to the uttermost, it is wholly new for an ulterior service . . . every end is converted into a new means." Emerson helped me see the more profound effects of a relationship to the land—of the spiritual dimensions and the poetic qualities. Of the behind-the-scenes power of being in connection with the land.

Sigurd Olson grew up in northern Wisconsin and is probably best known for helping to protect the Boundary Waters Canoe Area Wilderness in northern Minnesota. For each of twenty-five years I have spent a week in late summer with one or more family members canoeing in the Boundary Waters. Reading Olson's *Listening Point*, my favorite of his books, I am reminded of my adventures there. Olson wrote, "Campsites in the north are chosen for the things you can see at a distance, a landing for the canoe and outfit and place for the tent. But they are loved and remembered for the things you cannot see." Like Thoreau, Olson grasped the importance of a escaping to a sacred place, to a cabin in the woods or on a lake, a place away from the sounds and fury of everyday life, a place for contemplation and discovery.

In summer our pond
attracts all manner of
creatures.

Rachel Carson's *Silent Spring* awakened many to the powerful aftereffects of pesticides such as DDT. I was working for the UW Extension in Green Bay when *Silent Spring* hit the best-seller lists in the early 1960s. I was impressed with Carson's research and her vision, but I was in awe that a scientist could write in an understandable, even lyrical way. She wrote, "The history of life on earth has been a history of interaction between living things and their surroundings." Such common sense, yet so often ignored.

Of course, I knew of Gaylord Nelson as a Wisconsin senator (1949–1959) and governor (1959–1963) and admired his work in preserving the environment. I met him when he wrote an introduction to my first book, *The Land Still Lives*, published in 1970, and I followed his career and work closely. Nelson also served in the U.S. Senate from 1963 to 1981. During one of his first Senate speeches, in 1963, he said, "We need a comprehensive and nationwide program to save the national resources of America. We cannot be blind to the growing crisis of our environment. Our soil, our water, and our air are becoming more polluted every day. Our most priceless natural resources—trees, lakes, rivers, wildlife habitats, scenic landscapes— are being destroyed."

Nelson turned the attention of thousands, maybe millions, toward the importance of preserving the environment. He is perhaps best known as the founder of Earth Day, April 22. At a rally I attended during Earth Week in spring of 1970, more than two thousand University of Wisconsin students gave Senator Nelson a standing ovation at the beginning and end of his talk—a rare thing for university students to do in those days. At the rally Nelson said, "Our goal is an environment of decency, equality, and mutual respect for all other human beings and all other creatures. An environment without ugliness, without ghettos, without discrimination, without hunger, without poverty, and without war."

~~~~~~

All of these influences—dreams of escaping the turmoil of the city and introducing my children to a lifestyle I'd grown up with, an awareness that my parents would soon move to town, my lifelong interest in nature and the environment—helped make clear in a simple but compelling way the desire for a piece of land to call my own.

Then one day in the fall of 1964, while he was at the courthouse in Wautoma, my dad learned that the Coombes place was for sale, an abandoned farm no more than two miles south of our home place. The land had been abandoned after a disastrous fire in 1959 and had come up for sale when Mrs. Coombes died earlier in 1964 at the age of eighty-eight. One weekend when I was home, Dad asked me what I thought about him buying the place. The price, he said, essentially covered the back taxes owed.

I was elated. The Coombes farm was smaller than the home place, only a hundred acres, but in some ways it was more interesting because it included a five-acre pond. Although our home farm boasted twenty acres of woods, it was on high ground with no stream or pond.

When I was a boy, it was customary on Sunday afternoons to walk not only on our land but on the neighbors' as well. In those days there weren't any No Trespassing signs; we could walk almost anywhere, and we did. I remembered walking to the Coombes place with Dad one fall day. As we approached the pond, wild ducks lifted from the water—a huge flock, as I recall. The Coombes farm also had paper birch trees, and black willow, and black locust—we had none of those in our woods two miles away. The home farm was hilly, but not nearly so much so as the Coombes place. That in itself was interesting; you never know what's on the other side of a hill.

My dad knew I wanted land, and my brothers, Darrel and Don, had similar interests. And Dad also wanted a place for himself, a place where he could escape from "all those people" in town, where he knew he and my mother would move in a few years. In those days Wild Rose boasted about six hundred people—a crowd to Dad, who was accustomed to having no neighbors closer than a half mile. Dad wanted a place where he could watch the sun rise and set, unencumbered by buildings, electric lines, or other man-made obstacles. He wanted to look to the horizon and not see another person.

In 1964 Dad bought the Coombes property, as much for himself and my mother as for my brothers and me. In 1966 he sold the property to Darrel, Don, and me for one dollar.

Some forty years later, Roshara has become a touchstone in all our lives, a place where we have both discovered and maintained our connections to the land, a place where my three children and now their children have gained an appreciation for the land that transcends anything conveyed by a textbook, a film, or a video.

In 1966 our three children were of preschool age. In 2006 Susan, who lives in Madison, has two children: Josh, fourteen, and Ben, ten. Steve, who spent several years in Florida, and his partner, Natasha, also live in Madison. Jeff and his wife, Sandy, live in Colorado with their three children: Christian, nine; Nicholas, seven; and Elizabeth, two.

All of them are part of this story.

Prairie grasses and wildflowers in late fall

Chapter 2

∞∞∞∞∞∞∞∞∞∞∞∞∞∞∞∞

Skunk's Hollow

"Can't grow much more than sand burs. Tough place to make a living."
HERMAN APPS

After Dad had purchased the Coombes farm, I remembered that the community where the farm was located had the less-than-auspicious name "Skunk's Hollow." When I asked Dad how the area got its name, he shrugged as if to say it should be obvious. (I suspect that with the several small ponds in the area, there may have been more skunks than usual.)

When I was five or six years old, Dad drove me to a farm near ours that had once been owned by my Grandpa Apps. This 160-acre farm, already abandoned by the late 1930s, was about a mile southwest of the Coombes farm. Rambling along in our 1930s Willys car, we passed through Skunk's Hollow. We crossed hard-surfaced County Highway A and drove past the Chain O' Lake School, with its red woodshed and outhouses, one in each corner of the school lot. The sandy road twisted around Chain O' Lake and then climbed again, passing the Coombes place on the right and the Floyd Jeffers farm on the left. "Poor farms," Dad said. "Sandy farms—can't grow much more than sand burs. Tough place to make a living."

These were Depression years, and it was difficult for anyone to make a living no matter where they lived or how good their farms. Those who lived on the poorer farms especially suffered.

"Farm folks with little money live off their vegetable gardens," Dad told me. "They've got milk and butter from their cows, and they usually butcher a hog in the fall. They don't go hungry. Biggest problem they got is paying their taxes every year, and if they got a mortgage on their farm, then they really got a problem." I surely didn't understand everything my dad was telling me, but I could tell who lived poor just by looking: buildings without paint, skinny livestock, worn-out farm implements rusting in the yard.

On top of a rise beyond the Jeffers farm, we turned on a road leading west and dropped down to go around Wagner's Lake and Wagner's farm, then climbed to the top of another hill where Dad stopped the car next to a clump of huge cottonwood trees.

"This is Grandpa's old farm," Dad said. The barn had disappeared, but the old house, long abandoned, stood tucked against an oak woodlot that led to a pond a short hike down the hill.

The house had never been painted, but there was a certain beauty to the old gray boards, cracked and curled from years of blistering summer heat and frigid winters. The windows were broken, and the kitchen door hung by one hinge. A huge lilac bush stood to one side of the back door, and a box elder tree had grown through the broken boards of the front porch.

For a long time we stood looking at this weathered old house and listening to the breeze rustling the cottonwood leaves and inhaling the smells of summer. I wondered why we were standing there, doing nothing, but I stood quietly next to Dad, holding his hand and wondering what he was seeing that I couldn't see. I learned a valuable lesson that day. When two people look at the same thing, they often see something quite different.

When I was older I knew what Dad saw that day. He saw his mother and father, his brothers, Fred, Ed, George, and John, and his sisters, Doris, Irene, Elsie, and Minnie. It looked like an old house to me, a forgotten farm with trees growing where cattle once grazed. But to Dad it was much more. It was a place with meaning, a place with memories.

Dad pushed aside the kitchen door, and we walked among the clutter of broken glass, fallen plaster, and scraps of wallpaper hanging loose from the walls. In what had been the kitchen, he showed me where the cookstove had once stood, where the stovepipe went into the chimney, where the kitchen table had been, where his mother and sisters had washed dishes, where they kept the pail for drinking water. As we walked through the dining room he pointed out the stairway to the upstairs where he and his brothers and sisters had slept.

Back outside again he told me stories about hunting squirrels and rabbits, and Canada geese and mallards when they came down from the north each fall. He told me about hoeing corn and making hay, about milking cows and walking to country school. About digging potatoes and raising rutabagas. For him, this old, abandoned farm was more than an unpainted house with a leaky roof and a tree growing through the front porch. It was more than tree-studded acres that once grew potatoes and corn, oats and rye and provided pasture land for a few broken-down milk cows. This old farm was part of who he was. It shaped his life in ways that he wasn't fully aware of. Yet he knew something of the power of this land, and he wanted me to experience it, too.

I didn't just become aware of Skunk's Hollow that day, a little of its history and mystique, a little about people once there and still there. That day I began to learn something about how a piece of land can shape a person—influence how he thinks and what he believes.

Looking back, that early memory of Skunk's Hollow and the visit to my grandfather's old farm made my father's purchase of the Coombes place even more compelling. In a way I was coming home, destined to learn some of what my grandfather and father had learned working these hilly acres.

Field road on the way to the prairie

Chapter 3

Terminal Moraine and Tension Zone

"The soil is generally not suited to corn or other row crops because of the high susceptibility to soil blowing and water erosion."

1985 SOIL SURVEY

Every piece of land has a story to tell: of buildings and fences, of crops and woodlots and weather, and of course of the people who lived on it. One of the earliest, most dramatic events that shaped our Skunk's Hollow farm was the last glacier. This huge sheet of ice began moving into what is now Wisconsin some twenty-five thousand years ago, pushing over the land, tearing, ripping, and burying everything in its path.[1] The great glacier that formed the state's topography had six lobes, all of which extended south but missed southwestern Wisconsin. The Green Bay Lobe formed our farm, created the hills and valleys, and in its retreat ten thousand years ago left behind stones of many sizes, shapes, and colors, from pebbles to some as big as automobiles.

The glacier also left behind a string of ponds: Wagner's Lake, then our pond, then an unnamed one to the north of us, and then the largest, named Chain O' Lake. These small lakes and ponds formed when huge chunks of buried ice melted, leaving water-filled depressions. None of these ponds has an inlet or outlet, but each is fed by springs and natural runoff.

Our land is part of a moraine, or ridge of glacial deposit, that extends north to Stevens Point and south to Rock County. The moraine marks the site where the glacier stopped its southward progression and began retreating. Just to the west of our place is the Glacial Lake Wisconsin Basin, a huge area that was once covered with meltwater from the many years' accumulation of ice. Today it is a vast, sandy, irrigated vegetable-growing area—flat as the surface of the lake it once was, compared to the hills and valleys of our farm. It is a massive source of water just a few feet below the surface. Eventually, as the ice continued to melt and Glacial Lake Wisconsin grew larger, a wall of water forced its way south, forming the Wisconsin Dells. The Wisconsin River, which flows about twenty-five miles west of our farm through this once lake, now flat land, is a reminder of the glacier's work.

UW–MADISON, DEPT. OF GEOGRAPHY, CARTOGRAPHY LAB

The Ice Age Trail, one of only eight National Scenic Trails in the United States, passes a short distance from the western edge of our property, providing a place for hikers and explorers to see firsthand evidence of the glacier's massive force and what it left behind.

Running north-south through the terminal moraine is a divide that splits the direction of the groundwater here as well as the direction of nearby streams and rivers. Two miles west of our farm, on the west side of the divide, water flows west to the Wisconsin River and then on to the Mississippi River and the Gulf of Mexico. At our farm, the rivers and streams flow east, eventually into Green Bay and on to the Atlantic Ocean. A landowner's well two miles west of our farm reaches water at twenty feet, and our well is sixty feet deep. But a neighbor living directly on the divide has to go more than two hundred feet to get water for his well.

Floyd Jeffers, who lived across the road from our farm all his life, once told me that we had the best water in Waushara County. There was truth to his statement; we tap into the aquifer at its beginning, before the water has an opportunity to pick up contaminants.

In 1913 the Wisconsin Geological and Natural History Survey published the results of a soil survey of Waushara County. The lead author wrote, "[Waushara County] is made up of numerous hills, pothole depressions and narrow, irregular ridges and valleys. The hills vary in height from 30 to 100 feet or more above the Wisconsin River Valley."[2]

According to the survey, our farm's topsoil consisted of light brown sand of medium texture with little organic material and low water-holding capacity. The real meaning of this: We've got poor soil that requires lots of rain before crops amount to anything.

More than seventy years later, the National Cooperative Soil Survey (College of Agriculture and Life Sciences, UW–Madison, and Soil Conservation Service) conducted its own soil survey of Waushara County in 1985–1986.[3] By this time the soil scientists had come up with new, more sophisticated ways to describe the poor soil in our area.

Art Peterson, longtime soil science professor at UW–Madison and a neighbor in Madison, prepared an updated soil survey for our farm in 2004. Art said we had five types of soil: Richford loamy sand (6–12 percent slope), Richford loamy sand (12–20 percent slope), Coloma loamy sand (6–12 percent slope), Okee loamy sand (12–20 percent slope), and Okee loamy sand (2–6 percent slope). The higher the percentage of slope, the hillier the land. Most of our farm falls within the Okee loamy sand category. Soil scientists in 1985 described it this way: "Surface area is a dark brown loamy sand about two inches thick. Subsoil extends to a depth of about sixty-inches. . . . Most areas are used as woodland. A few are used as cropland or pasture."[4]

Soil scientists classed some of our acres as Coloma loamy sand, describing it this way: "This sloping, excessively drained soil is on the sides of ridges and knolls on moraines. The soil is generally not suited to corn or other row crops because of the high susceptibility to soil blowing and water erosion."[5]

Knee-high sweet corn in the garden—and it's still June.

Over the years I have found one area on the farm where the soil is somewhat heavier than elsewhere, containing more organic material and with a stickier subsoil. The soil in this two-acre field doesn't fit any of the scientists' categories, as the soil contains a goodly amount of clay. Here's how I know. A few years ago, in April, I was plowing the small field near a white pine windbreak a couple hundred yards south of my cabin. The frost wasn't entirely out of the ground, especially on the north side of the windbreak, where my tractor became impossibly

Pine and black locust

stuck on a little knoll, sinking through the topsoil into the stickiest of sticky soils my tractor and I had ever encountered. It took me more than two hours to ease my little John Deere out of the sticky subsoil that sucked at my tractor's tires like quicksand.

Both the early and the more recent soil surveyors documented the crops growing in the area. Potatoes were the main crop in 1913, yielding 75 to 125 bushels per acre, up to 250 bushels per acre in a wet year and grown on the heavier soils. Other major crops were corn (20 to 35 bushels per acre), rye (10 bushels per acre), and navy beans (no yields reported).[6]

Where potatoes are grown today in the Town of Rose and in the townships to the west, yields were about 800 bushels per acre in 2004. Corn yields in 2004 and 2005 averaged about 130 bushels per acre.[7] The soil here hasn't changed, but agricultural practices have. Most of today's high yields result from irrigation and ample amounts of fertilizer.

Without irrigation, the relatively recent 1985 soil survey scientists said my predominantly Okee loamy sand soil should yield seventy bushels of corn per acre, sixty-five bushels of oats, three and a half tons of bromegrass alfalfa hay, or twenty-four bushels of soybeans. Of course, these yields assume a growing season of average rainfall. Because these sandy soils dry out so quickly, unless rain comes regularly throughout the growing season, yields are severely reduced, some years providing no crop at all.

The soil surveyors in 1985 recommended tree species for my Okee loamy sand. Hardwoods: northern pin oak and black oak. Coniferous: red pine, jack pine, and eastern white pine. All these tree species and more now grow on my farm. We have planted only the red pine; the rest have grown naturally.

Sometimes I hear visitors to our state claim that they pass through a "tension zone" when they drive through central Wisconsin and on into the state's northern vacationlands. They are usually referring to their mental state. But my farm rests near the middle of a true biological tension zone as well.[8]

This tension zone, defined by biologists, is an imaginary band twenty or thirty miles wide that passes through northwestern Wisconsin, then through the central part of the state, and on south, ending at Lake Michigan south of Sheboygan. Within this band, plant and animal species from northern and southern Wisconsin overlap. Bur oak grows in southern Wisconsin but not in the northern part of the state. White pine grows naturally in the north but not in the south. Black bear roam the north but not the south (although it appears bears are moving farther south each year due to loss of habitat). Yet we have bur oak, white pine, and black bears at our farm.

Amazingly, our farm is on the intersection of the terminal moraine and the biological tension zone. I tell my grandsons that because

UW–MADISON, DEPT. OF GEOGRAPHY, CARTOGRAPHY LAB

of this unusual coming together, our farm is a place where strange creatures can be found. We might discover exotic plants and animals and even buried gems transported from northern Canada. "Sure, Grandpa," the boys say.

But there is some truth behind the claims. Diamonds have been found in glacial leavings near Eagle in Waukesha County, southwest of Oregon in Dane County, and in Ozaukee, Racine, and Washington Counties. The largest weighed more than fifteen carats. As long ago as 1670 Jesuit fathers told stories of diamonds found on several islands at the entrance to Green Bay.[9]

Aside from the skepticism about tension zones and terminal moraines, land at this intersection does provide interesting perspectives beyond the tall tales.

Chapter 4

◇◇◇◇◇◇◇◇◇◇◇◇◇◇◇◇◇◇◇◇

Surveys, Maps, and First People

"This Township is mostly made up of a high ridge of barren hills on which there is very little timber, but which are covered with a stunted growth of black oak brush."

SURVEYOR IRA COOK

The view west from the prairie

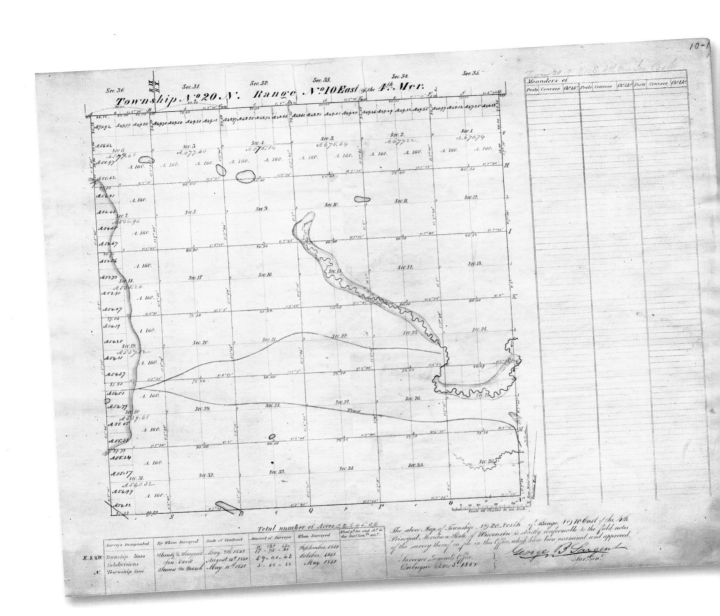

May 1851 survey map for the Town of Rose, showing section numbers

COURTESY OF THE WISCONSIN BOARD OF COMMISSIONERS OF PUBLIC LANDS

Long before soil scientists declared my land marginal for farming, federal government surveyors said the same thing. G. R. Stuntz and J. O. Sargent worked their way across northern Waushara County in May 1851, conducting what was called an "exterior survey," which divided the county into townships.[1] With their survey team, which consisted of two chainmen (John Sinclair and Elisha Whitney) and two axmen (John Chisholm and Chester Coburn), they divided the county into eighteen townships and established the official township dividing lines. In their survey notes about what was to become Rose Township, Stuntz and Sargent wrote, "Surface rolling, soil sandy, second rate. No timber. Oak brush, willow and grass."[2] Not a glowing report.

On October 2, 1851, Ira Cook and his survey crew began an "interior survey" of the township that later became known as Rose.[3] Cook and his crew, consisting of assistant surveyor John Rogan, four chainmen (J. B. Salisbury, J. B. Potter, C. B. McLaughlin, and Daniel Gallager), and two axmen (S. Wright and George Wier), established section (640 acres) and quarter-section (160 acres) boundaries within the townships.

Imagine what it must have been like for a survey crew to enter what was still wild country. They had no nearby town for provisions, no roof over their heads on rainy nights except a canvas tent. They camped their way through the countryside, measuring and making maps and writing notes about what they saw. Not many miles to the south, farmers grew wheat by the hundreds of acres, but in this new territory there was nothing but sandy, rock-strewn hills, some open prairie, and black oaks and white oaks.

Like Stuntz and Sargent, Ira Cook didn't think much of the land that is now our farm. Nor did he have much positive to say about the township where the farm is located. He wrote, "This Township is mostly made up of a high ridge of barren hills on which there is very little

A page from Ira Cook's survey notes describing our land, 1851

COURTESY OF THE WISCONSIN BOARD OF COMMISSIONERS OF PUBLIC LANDS timber, but which are covered with a stunted growth of black oak brush. There is very little arable land in the township. . . . The eastern part of the township, however [words not legible] and contains some good soil. Where the land is at all adapted to cultivation, the soil is first rate. . . . [There] are several small lakes and ponds, and one small creek [now known as the Upper Pine River] that rises in Section 10 and runs in a southeast course through the township."[4] Cook also noted that the hills here were filled with "granite boulders."

These survey crews may have been the first nonnative visitors to much of Rose Township. That October of 1851 Cook wrote in his leather-bound log book, ". . . the township . . . as yet contains no settlers."[5] Of course, native people had spent thousands of years on these lands, trapping, tapping maple trees, and hunting.

The government survey that divided most of the United States into townships, sections, and quarter sections resulted from the Federal Land Ordinances of 1784, 1785, and 1787 and the Land Act of 1796. The survey excluded the original thirteen states, Vermont, Texas, Hawaii, parts of southern California, and parts of Maine. Many of those states used the British metes and bounds system, which described property lines based on what the eye could see—and often included in property descriptions such landmarks as trees, rivers, and other physical features that could and did change over time.

The U.S. government survey of which our farm is a part began in 1785 at the Pennsylvania border with Ohio and proceeded westward. Native American tribes occupied most of these lands at the time, so before the federal government could survey and sell the lands it "negotiated" treaties with the tribes. In most cases the government forced these treaties upon the Indians, creating untold strife and unhappiness among the native peoples who had lived on these lands for centuries.

At the heart of this tragic conflict was differing approaches to the land. Owning land was a European-American idea, at odds with Native American philosophies of sharing vast areas of land. Before whites arrived, the idea of individuals owning a piece of ground was largely eschewed by these early peoples who lived on what is now our farm.

In Wisconsin, much of the land west of Lake Poygan, north of the Fox River, and east of the Wisconsin River had been Menominee Indian territory until 1848. In that year, the year Wisconsin became a state, the Menominee ceded the last of their land to the United States in the Treaty of Lake Poygan (Lake Pow-aw-hay-kon-nay), signed on October 18. The treaty, ratified January 23, 1849, promised the Menominee a new homeland of 600,000 acres in

Minnesota, plus $350,000—$150,000 for moving expenses and the remaining $200,000 to be paid in equal cash installments over ten years beginning in 1857. The Menominee could continue to live in Wisconsin until 1850.[6] In 1847 the Menominee tribe included about twenty-five hundred people. Of that number it is estimated that twenty-two hundred lived by hunting and fishing and three hundred were farmers. Most of those farming lived near Lake Poygan.[7]

Shortly after the treaty was negotiated in 1848, Chief Oshkosh and several other Menominee chiefs visited the new land in Minnesota; they liked neither the close proximity to the Crow Wing tribe nor the quality of the land. When the representatives returned in 1849, they immediately sent a delegation from the tribe to Washington. Chief Oshkosh made an impassioned speech to President Millard Fillmore, arguing the Menominees' displeasure with the 1848 treaty. According to a translation of his speech, Chief Oshkosh "preferred . . . a home somewhere in Wisconsin, for the poorest region of Wisconsin was better than that of the Crow Wing."[8] In 1852 President Fillmore granted the Menominee a temporary reservation along the Wolf River.

In May 1854 the Menominee, with the consent of the Wisconsin legislature, signed another treaty making the reservation permanent and giving up the promised Minnesota lands. In addition, the federal government would pay the Menominee $242,686 over fifteen years starting in 1857 to cover the difference between the original 600,000 acres they were promised and the 276,480 acres they would now own (and which is now Menomonee County). For all of their millions of acres of Wisconsin lands, the tribe received on average about thirteen cents an acre in payment.[9]

Wisconsin lands were surveyed between 1833 and 1866. Surveyors established the baseline and meridian in 1832 and then began work in southern Wisconsin, starting at the Wisconsin-Illinois border and a point about ten miles east of the Mississippi River. This Point of Beginnings was the intersection of the state's border with Illinois and the Fourth Principal Meridian. This meridian extends north from the mouth of the Illinois River, between the Grant and Iowa County line, and then through Richland, Vernon, Monroe, Jackson, Clark, Taylor, Price, Ashland, and Iron Counties to Lake Superior.[10]

East-west lines crossing the principal meridian every six miles are township lines. The township numbers reflect how far north a location is from the baseline (the Illinois border) and how far east or west from the Fourth Principal Meridian. Our farm is located twenty townships north of the Illinois border and ten townships east of the Fourth Principal Meridian. Thus the land description of our farm begins: Township 20 North, Range 10 East.

According to standard procedure, surveyor Ira Cook numbered the thirty-six sections, each consisting of 640 acres, starting in the upper right (northeast) corner of the township with number 1 and moving across with section number 36 in the lower right (southeast) corner. Our farm is located in section 33, which is in the bottom row of sections in Rose Township (30 through 36) and near the township boundary line that separates Rose from Wautoma Township to the south.

With the sections properly marked, the survey crew continued to locate quarter sections of 160 acres each, which became a standard farm size for many Midwestern settlers. The complete and official location of our farm in survey language is the "north one half of the southwest one quarter of section 33, township 20 north, range 10 east (80 acres), plus the south twenty (20 acres) of the northwest quarter of section 33, township 20 north, range 10 east, Waushara County, Wisconsin, total acreage, 100." The original parcel was 160 acres, but Tom Stewart, the first owner, sold 60 northern acres in 1877. By knowing the surveyors' land description, I can quickly determine that our farm is twenty townships (20 x 6 miles) or 120 miles from the Illinois border, as the crow flies. Likewise, if we are range 10 east, I know we are 60 miles (10 x 6 miles) from the Fourth Principal Meridian. Straight west of us, the Fourth Meridian passes through Monroe and Jackson Counties.

Surveyor Cook wrote about section 33 and the land that comprises our farm: "Surface hilly. Soil second rate. Timber black, bur and white oak with undergrowth of black oak . . . and hazel brush." In comments about sections 27 and 28, which lie just to the north of our farm, he wrote, "Indian trail bears west."[11] Today County Highway A follows this early Native American route through the area. This county road is now one of the main routes to Wild Rose, the closest village to our farm.

Cook made no mention of meeting Indians as his crew worked across the township, but the Indian trails that he marked on his map continued to be used well into the late 1800s and long after the land was supposedly settled.

With its land survey completed, the U.S. government could now sell the land based on survey descriptions. Land buyers didn't need to step foot on a property to buy it, although most would want to. Even with section 33 surveyed, there were no immediate takers—understandable,

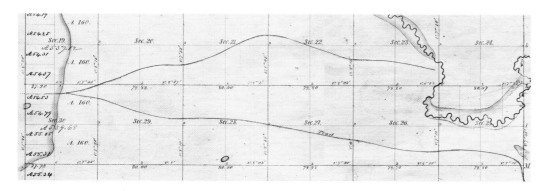

A closeup of the 1851 survey map shows Indian trails crossing Rose Township.
COURTESY OF THE WISCONSIN BOARD OF COMMISSIONERS OF PUBLIC LANDS

because the better land in the township was to the north and east. Checking the Wisconsin Land Patents Database, I learned that Josiah Etheredge and John Etheridge (perhaps relatives, with one name misspelled in the records?) each obtained a land patent in 1855 for eighty acres in sections 25 and 26, just west of present-day Wild Rose. Cornelius Etheridge bought a land patent for forty acres in 1856 and another for forty acres in 1858. Daniel Davies bought eighty acres in section 24 in 1855. Samuel Patterson bought forty acres in section 12 in 1857. That same year, Martin A. Redfield bought forty acres in section 12. Richard Roberts bought forty acres in section 12 in 1857, forty acres in 1858, and another forty in 1861.[12]

But our section 33 sat idle until after the Civil War, which says something about the poor quality of the land, its hills and stony fields. Thomas Stewart acquired what is now my farm in 1867. Milan Jeffers bought a land patent for 160 acres in section 33 in 1873, land directly across the road from my farm. James Jeffers bought the quarter section north of Milan Jeffers in 1874. Remnants of James Jeffers's homestead buildings—stone walls—are still visible.[13]

Who were these early pioneers who ended up on what turned out to be one of the poorest farms in a township of many poor, sandy farms?

Showy goldenrod on the prairie

Chapter 5

◇◇◇◇◇◇◇◇◇◇◇◇◇◇◇◇◇

Early Settlers

"Father remarked that wheat was never again as yellow and abundant
as the first harvest they raised."

JOHN WOODWARD

The earliest recorded story about pioneer settlement on the lands around our farm is a handwritten autobiography by John M. Woodward, who was born November 11, 1852, on a farm a mile or so south of our place.[1] Woodward's parents moved from New Hampshire to central Wisconsin in March 1851. They arrived by boat at Sheboygan and then traveled over land to Greenbush, Fond du Lac, Berlin (a trading post on the Fox River), and finally Wautoma. The senior Woodward referred to the area as "Indian land," as indeed it was. John Woodward was born a year later in a shanty built of rough boards hauled some six miles from a "crude sawmill" in Wautoma to the land his father had selected. The rustic home was about twelve feet by twelve feet, with cracks "chinked and battened" to keep out the wet and cold.

John Woodward wrote about his father's recollections of the Indians in the area. "The Menominee tribe of Indians ranged the country around us, led by Menominee John, a splendid specimen of savage standing six feet in his moccasins with long black hair and a long nose."[2]

The Woodward family lived in Indian country for but one year before returning to New Hampshire. Woodward wrote, "It was the isolation, loneliness, and homesickness that caused them to return east. As far as I can recall from what they said, they made little progress that first year beyond building their shanty and raising a garden from seeds they brought with them. For one thing, they raised a great abundance of melons. Such melons as the virgin soil produced were never raised after the country was settled and the ground used for other purposes. Father remarked that wheat was never again as yellow and abundant as the first harvest they raised."

The Woodward family soon returned to Wisconsin, this time with a second son, who had been born in New Hampshire. Some seventy years later, John Woodward described their lives in the 1850s and 1860s:

The Indians were our nearest neighbors who called most frequently. Deer were seen more than squirrels are now. Venison was the only "beef." I remember in childhood wild meat was the only meat except when pigs were killed in the fall. Bears were often seen, and sometimes killed, but generally not until they had robbed the pig pens. All cattle were saved for cows and oxen. Ox teams were the only ones and only the most fortunate settlers had these.

In the spring passenger pigeons filled the air and often made it as dark as on a cloudy day. Men had to patrol their newly seeded fields with guns every morning and often at other times. I went up and down a field many times keeping pigeons and other wild fowl off.

Prairie hens flew up before us wherever we went. Flocks of wild geese would light and strut over the fields. Millions of game fowl were killed every year, the breast cut out and the rest thrown away. The exceptions were the wild geese and ducks which were fit in their season.

But the poorest people of today [Woodward was writing in the 1920s] know nothing of the poverty of that early time in spite of the abundance of nature. There were no luxuries to be had, if they had the money, and the necessities of today were luxuries then, beyond the reach of all because they were unobtainable.

Only the cheapest grade of cloth was sold in the stores. Many wives of the pioneers spun the flax and wool into yarn after their husbands had broken the flax and carded the wool by hand, and then wove their clothing on primitive looms.

Boots from cowhide were the finest things worn by men. . . . Many mothers bound their children's feet in rags in cold weather.

Cornbread, johnnycake and mush were staple foods together with potatoes and rye bread. Wheat and flour were scarcer and conserved more carefully than during the World War [World War I].

There was pork at killing time for those who were enterprising and thrifty enough to raise pigs and fortunate enough to save them from wild animals. And there was milk and butter when the cows came in (a calf was born and the cow once more gave milk).

The prairie in early fall

Our treat for company was turnips. We would bring up a basket of them. All would sit around and talk and scrape turnips until 12 o'clock or often later. Then before separating they would have a session of prayer and sing the old hymns sung in the east or even in England.[3]

Living conditions challenged the sturdiest of the settlers who lived in Waushara County and the Township of Rose in the late 1850s through the 1860s. These were the conditions that Thomas Stewart, the first pioneer owner of our land, faced when he arrived in 1867.

When Tom Stewart farmed these acres, he made hay by cutting it and then drying it in little piles, sometimes called haycocks. He hauled the dry hay to his barn, where he stored it for winter feed.

Chapter 6

Tom Stewart

"[A]ny person who is the head of a family, or who has arrived at the age of twenty-one years, and is a citizen of the United States, . . . shall from and after the first of January, eighteen hundred and sixty-three, be entitled to enter one quarter section or a less quantity of unappropriated public lands. . . ."

THE HOMESTEAD ACT, 1862

At the height of the Civil War, on May 20, 1862, the U.S. Congress passed the Homestead Act. President Lincoln signed it into law that same year. The law—whose purpose, of course, was to encourage settlement of land in the west—declared "[t]hat any person who is the head of a family, or who has arrived at the age of twenty-one years, and is a citizen of the United States, or who shall have filed his declaration of intention to become such, as required by the naturalization laws of the United States, and who has never borne arms against the United States Government or given aid and comfort to its enemies, shall from and after the first of January, eighteen hundred and sixty-three, be entitled to enter one quarter section or a less quantity of unappropriated public lands. . . ." Those who met these requirements, who lived on and cultivated their parcel for a minimum of five years, and who paid a small filing fee, were eligible for a quarter section, or 160 acres, at no cost. The act gave priority to Union veterans, who could deduct the number of years served in the war from the five-year residency requirement. (As the language of the law made clear: Confederate soldiers need not apply.)

The land that would become our farm remained in government ownership until 1867, two years after the end of the war. While other farms had begun to spring up in the township of Rose, our land, with its sandy soil and steep hills, remained much as it was when the last great glacier formed it ten thousand years ago. But in 1866 Union veteran Tom Stewart, a

New York native whose family moved to Waushara County sometime before the Civil War, returned to Wisconsin to look for homestead lands. Several of his friends from New York lived in Rose Township, and he soon found an eligible quarter section here, in section 33.

Civil War veteran Tom Stewart, the farm's first owner
COURTESY OF PAM ANDERSON, MADISON

Thomas Jefferson Stewart, the son of Solomon J. Stewart and Sally Ann Stewart, was born March 4, 1846, on a farm near Rose, New York. Tom's family had joined other New York friends in Springwater Township in Waushara County sometime between 1852 and 1860. Tom volunteered for duty in the Civil War on January 18, 1864, when he was not quite eighteen years old, and became a part of the 35th Regiment Infantry, Company F.[1]

Civil War records indicate that Tom was injured five months later. Sergeant William Striedy reported: "On the 15th of June, 1864, while in the line of duty and without fault or improper conduct on his part, at or near Port Hudson, State of Louisiana said soldier [Thomas Stewart] incurred an injury or strain while he was assisting in loading the wagons containing the Regimental equipment on to a boat to go to Morgan Bend, Louisiana. He was working with a detail of men under my charge when the wheels of one of the wagons dropped off the gang plank and he was lifting to help get it back on again. Then all at once, I saw he was hurt in some way by his looks and he said, 'Sir, I am hurt; it makes me sick.' I told him he had better go on the boat and lie down, which he did. When we got to Morganzia, I took him to the regimental hospital and [he] was afterward sent to hospital at New Orleans."[2]

Tom Stewart was in a New Orleans hospital again from August 10 through 15, 1864, this time with diarrhea "caused by drinking Mississippi River water . . . and marsh water there being no other to have at that time."[3] Tom was sick again in September and October of 1864 and was absent from his military duties. He recovered enough to continue serving with his unit and was mustered out on March 15, 1866, at Brownsville, Texas.[4] Tom received a disability pension of four dollars per month "on account of disease of urinary organs."

Tom Stewart turned twenty-one in March 1867 and staked his claim on April 30. The Homestead Act required that Tom move onto his property within six months of filing his claim. He had to build a house—a log cabin would suffice—and he had to actively farm the property, which meant growing crops. Thanks to his two years of military duty, he would own his land in only three years if he met these requirements.[5]

Tom built a cabin and other buildings on the south side of the wagon trail that split the quarter section in half. He started clearing land that first spring. Much of the sandy acres were covered with black oak, hazel brush, and stunted oak. Big bluestem grass grew in the open areas, as tall as a man in many places. Big bluestem sends its roots deep into the sandy soil, allowing it to reach moisture and withstand the dry, hot summers common in this part of Wisconsin. With his team of oxen, Tom pulled out the smaller oak trees, first shoveling soil away from the bottom of each tree until the tangled mass of roots was exposed and then hooking a heavy logging chain around each trunk and to the ox yoke. Slowly the chain tightened as the oxen pushed into their yokes. The oak roots cracked as the animals strained, and the stunted oak slowly tipped over and emerged from the sandy soil.

When he had several trees dug out, Tom dragged them into huge piles and set them ablaze. The smoke from Tom Stewart's fires could be seen for miles around, but no one was concerned. Many other farmers were clearing land they had purchased from the government. Everyone was burning brush and trees.

When he had a patch of ground cleared, Tom hired the team of Ike Woodward and William Henry Jenks, who went from farm to farm with their breaking plow and oxen to open new land. The two partners each owned two yoke of oxen (eight animals total), and together they owned the massive breaking plow, which had a white oak beam two feet thick and eighteen feet long, strong enough to absorb the shock of the plow hitting stones and tree roots. The plow's moldboard was five feet long and cut a furrow

Big bluestem grass covered much of the farm before the land was first plowed.

twenty inches wide and eight or nine inches deep through the virgin soil. This moldboard was constructed to turn over soil never before disturbed—and big bluestem sod, with its thick, tough tangle of roots, was especially difficult to plow. (Farmers used a short, less powerful moldboard plow once the land was broken.)

Plow. Wt., 63 lbs. Price $5.75
No. 32K421 14-Inch Rod Breaking
Plow. Wt., 64 lbs. Price $5.95
No. 32K422 16-Inch Rod Breaking
Plow. Wt., 67 lbs. Price $6.15

value ever offered in a gang plow. We fur
stubble shape. When ordering specify whic
neckyoke, weed hooks, two rolling coulters a
No. 32K410 12-Inch Gang Plow.
No. 32K411 14-Inch Gang Plow.

OUR WONDER VALUE PRAIRIE BREAKING PLOWS.

$7 37

This is the most popular style of Prairie Breaking Plow
on the market and is too well known to need further description. Price is for the plow complete, as shown in the
illustration and with one extra share. We
will furnish plow with gauge wheel and
rolling coulter for $1.85 extra.
No. 32K425 12-Inch Prairie Breaking Plow. Wt. 135 lbs. Price . . $7.37
No. 32K426 14-Inch Prairie Breaking Plow. Wt., 137 lbs. Price . . $7.65
No. 32K427 16-Inch Prairie Breaking Plow. Wt., 140 lbs. Price . . $7.85

Settlers used this type of breaking plow to turn grassy, never-before-plowed prairies.
SEARS, ROEBUCK CATALOG, 1908, FROM THE AUTHOR'S COLLECTION

The breaking plow was sturdy—and so were the plowmen. Woodward and Jenks took turns holding the plow day after day, from early spring until freeze-up, as they broke new land on farms all over Rose Township.

It took ten oxen to pull the plow. When they came to Tom Stewart's homestead, Jenks and Woodward hooked their oxen to the plow and added Tom Stewart's pair. The plow slowly turned the heavy sod, leaving golden-brown soil ready for the harrow and drag. The fresh smell of newly broken soil hinted at the untapped productivity and crops—especially wheat and potatoes—that would grow where once there was prairie and scrub oak.

Tom Stewart cleared enough land that first year to make a living from his crops. His main crop was likely wheat. Wheat was the premier crop throughout central and southern Wisconsin back as far as the 1840s, when large numbers of New Englanders and northern European immigrants began pouring into the state. The rich, never-before-plowed land yielded as much as twenty to twenty-five bushels per acre. Wisconsin rose from being the nation's ninth wheat producer in 1850 to second in 1860.[6]

But by the late 1860s Wisconsin's wheat production had begun an irrevocable decline. Many of the pioneers from New England and upper New York State had come to Wisconsin because of depleted agricultural lands back east; now these pioneer farmers were doing the same

Wisconsin farmers harvesting wheat with an early reaper, photographed in the 1870s by Andreas Larsen Dahl

Tom Stewart married Maria Jenks on August 28, 1869.

CERTIFICATE OF MARRIAGE, TOM STEWART AND MARIA JENKS, REGISTER OF DEEDS,
WAUSHARA COUNTY, WAUTOMA, WISCONSIN

thing in Wisconsin. They plowed up huge expanses of land—forty-acre fields and more—and planted the land with wheat year after year. Large wheat fields on central Wisconsin's sandy soil posed a particular problem: dry weather combined with westerly winds caused severe wind erosion; the topsoil literally was moved off the fields in huge clouds of dust. Wheat yields after repeated years of growing the crop often plummeted to five or six bushels per acre.[7]

Although there are no records about Tom Stewart's success or failure at growing wheat, the evidence of soil erosion on our farm is everywhere, evident in the humps of soil piled up along former fencerows. The first of the erosion no doubt occurred soon after this hilly, sandy land was plowed.

By 1869 Tom was well established, and he married Maria Jenks, daughter of neighbors John T. and Polly Jenks, on August 28 of that year.[8] Now Tom had someone to help him in the fields, to prepare his meals, to share his disappointments and fortunes. A baby boy, William, was born November 14, 1870. Another son, Irven, was born in 1874 but lived less than a year. The Stewarts would have three more children.

Satisfied with the improvements Tom had made on the land, the government granted him a land patent on August 1, 1874, which gave him clear title to his 160 acres.[9] The farm was his. The same year, the nearby village was organized and named Wild Rose to avoid confusion with Rose Township. The many wild roses growing in the vicinity made the name romantically appropriate.

TOM STEWART

On a shopping day, Tom and Maria would likely have hitched their team to their wagon, headed north about a mile down the dusty road to the old Indian trail (now County Highway A), and then turned east for about four miles to Wild Rose, along the Pine River. The town was founded in 1872 with a store and post office. By 1875 seventy-three families lived in Rose Township.[10] The population of the village of Wild Rose at that time is unknown.

A June 1875 article in the *Waushara Argus* noted:

Wild Rose was started about two years ago by J. H. Jones, who established a store upon a portion of the John Davies farm and procured a post office. [Now] the village . . . has two well filled stores, the proprietors of each of which reported a good business this spring.

The Grangers [a national farm organization] were putting up the frame to their new hall. Mr. Lincoln last year established a blacksmith shop here. He has associated himself with a wagon maker and the two kinds of business will be carried on in his shop. Nearby the village is Pine River, which is said to be a large enough stream to make a very good mill power. The country near is very good wheat country. As it is eight miles to the nearest mill, a grist mill would be a great convenience, but the probability of its paying might be questioned. [A water-powered grist and sawmill was built circa 1875.] The people [living in the village at the time] are mostly Welsh, steady, industrious, frugal and accommodating fellows, who generally live in good frame houses, well painted, with everything about them indicating thrift and progress.[11]

Tom and Maria Stewart lived among neighbors who spoke Norwegian (the Nelsons, Knutsons, Olsons, Keups), Polish (Ciesielskis, Gabrilskas, Hudziaks, Kowalaskis, Musinskis, Osinskis, Swendrzynskis, Wikowskis, Wajeiihowskis), and German (Handrichs, Apps, Witts, Kepplers, Esherhuts). A story is told in these parts about a German farmer who needed a new wooden box for his farm wagon. He knew his Norwegian neighbor was a carpenter, but the two men could not understand each other. The German farmer used a stick to draw a picture of a wagon box in the dirt. The Norwegian neighbor nodded to indicate he understood and soon had constructed a fine new wagon box for his neighbor.

Norwegian settlers organized a Lutheran church a few miles south of Wild Rose in 1862. And German immigrants organized a German Lutheran church that met in people's homes and in other churches until they built their own in 1941. Poles organized a Catholic church just to the north of Rose Township in Heffron.

The Stewarts likely were members of the Standalone Church, which once stood in front of the cemetery by the same name (now Mount Pleasant Cemetery), a mile south of Wild Rose. The Standalones were an unusual group of Christians who did not believe in denominational affiliation or organized church work. William Jeffers and several other Wild Rose pioneers brought the Standalone religion with them from Wayne County, New York, in the 1850s. Photographs at the Wild Rose Historical Society show that at least fifty local citizens belonged to the church at one time, including such names as Jenks, Jeffers, Pierce, and Darling. The Stewarts' neighbor Jim Jeffers was a member, as were Fred Jenks, who had land to the west of Tom Stewart's farm, and Maria Stewart's parents.

John Woodward, an early settler in the Wild Rose area and not a fan of the Standalones, wrote in his autobiography (circa 1925), "They were not a church. In fact they were fanatically opposed to all church organizations and systematic religious work. They believed in everyone standing alone and believing what he had a mind to. They dominated the religious influence of the community for years; their peculiarities persist in their descendents even today. . . . The Standalones opposed any preparation for the ministry or study for sermons as distrusting God and his power to help his servants. The cry was 'open your mouth and the Lord will fill it.' They believed that if God wanted a man to preach he would put into his mind what he wanted him to say."[12]

The Christian Church, built by John T. Jenks and John Etheridge Sr., and seating up to seventy members, opened its doors just west of Wild Rose in 1870. The church was about three miles west of the Standalone Church, considerably closer to the homes of many Standalone members. Many former Standalone members joined this new church, which led to the eventual demise of the Standalone Church.[13]

By 1903 most of the Christian Church members had joined other new churches in Wild Rose. A Methodist church began services in 1879, and a Baptist church opened in 1901.

THE STEWARTS

Tom Stewart died April 3, 1903. His wife, Maria, died January 3, 1927. Both are buried in Mount Pleasant Cemetery (formerly Standalone Cemetery), one mile south of Wild Rose, Wisconsin, on Highway 22. They had five children, four of whom were buried in Standalone Cemetery:

WILLIAM A. STEWART
  Born November 14, 1870
  Died March 5, 1899

IRVEN STEWART
  Born September 7, 1874
  Died June 1, 1875

INA LEONA STEWART
  Born April 23, 1876
  Died 1964

ARTHUR GARFIELD STEWART
  Born May 14, 1881
  Died July 18, 1953
  (burial place not known)

BENJAMIN HARRISON STEWART
  Born May 5, 1888
  Died 1941[14]

Most of the Welsh people (including the Jones, Davies, Hughes, Evans, Thomas, Owens, and Roberts families) who settled here belonged to a Presbyterian congregation that began as early as 1856.

Children in Tom Stewart's neighborhood attended the one-room Chain O' Lake School, a little wooden building about a mile north of the Stewart farm. Imagine the challenge of teaching a room full of exuberant youngsters who spoke several languages but knew little if any English. (I attended this same one-room school for eight years, starting in 1939.)

The glue that held this diverse group of farmers together was the understanding that they must get along if they hoped to survive in this rather unforgiving land of sandy and stony hills, where a rainfall or two could determine whether they had a crop in a given year. Tom Stewart and his Yankee friends, like their immigrant neighbors, knew that this new land required cooperation and a "caring for each other" perspective.

Sometime before 1877 (the title record is not specific), Tom Stewart sold sixty acres off the north side of his farm to B. E. Darling. This segment was almost entirely wooded, very hilly and stony, and included portions of two ponds. On October 3, 1877, Tom Stewart sold his remaining one hundred acres to Laura Hursh for $650, and he and his family moved away. I found them in the 1880 census living in Deerfield Township, which is a few miles west of our farm and boasts fewer hills and stones. Tom Stewart likely moved on to a more profitable farm.

Woven wire fence once formed a lane for livestock to travel from the Coombeses' barnyard to the pond.

Chapter 7

John, Ina, and Weston Coombes

"Another night like the last one and we'll be buyin' new thermometers."

INA COOMBES

After Tom Stewart sold out and moved away, a long succession of owners worked our farm for a few years and moved on. Joseph and Laura Hursh, who bought one hundred acres in 1877, sold to William Hursh in 1886, who sold to George P. Walker in 1900.[1] By that year, sixteen years after its founding, Wild Rose had eighty residents and boasted a water-powered gristmill and a school. One writer noted, "Charles A. Smart is postmaster and proprietor of the only general store. The mill is owned by James Larson. Mrs. Mary Gordon keeps a hotel. George A. Sage has a blacksmith and wagon shop, S. G. Abbott is resident physician and dentist."[2]

George P. Walker sold the farm to T. H. Patterson in 1904. Patterson, a land investor and Civil War veteran, had built a new fifty-by-one-hundred-foot, two-story brick store in Wild Rose in 1900. It was the largest building in the village.

There is no evidence that Patterson ever lived on the property he bought from Walker. Philo Darling, under a land contract (a lease arrangement) to Patterson, moved onto the place in the spring of 1904. That April, Wild Rose was incorporated as a village.[3] By the following year, eight Chicago and Northwestern passenger and freight trains would stop each day in Wild Rose, four heading north and four south.[4]

On January 17, 1904, T. H. Patterson sold the farm to D. R. Bowen for one thousand dollars. Bowen in turn entered into a land contract with Gordon Darling, who moved onto the

Main Street in Wild Rose, 1910
WHi IMAGE ID 35464

property. Apparently not thinking much of the place, or more probably running into financial difficulty, Darling transferred his land contract to Benjamin Stewart on October 23, 1908, after being on the place through only one growing season.[5] Benjamin Stewart was the youngest son of Tom Stewart, so the farm had returned to a member of the original family to settle here.

Wild Rose was continuing to grow, and the village board signed a contract on August 1, 1908, with the Rose Milling Company under which the gristmill would provide the village with electric streetlights. Soon after, most village residents had electricity, while rural residents would remain in the dark for many years to come, their lighting provided by candles, kerosene lamps, and lanterns.[6]

Benjamin Stewart worked the farm for nearly three years before he transferred the land contract to his sister Ina's husband, John Coombes, in 1911. (The title remained with D. R. Bowen.) Ina, at thirty-five a thin and quiet woman, and John, forty-three and a tall, soft-spoken, deliberate Englishman, had rented many farms in the neighborhood. Along with their children Charlotte, seventeen, and Weston, thirteen, the Coombeses had most recently been renting the John R. Jones farm, about two miles north of their new farm. (Another son, George, was born in 1900 but lived only eleven months.)

Coombes soon built a set of buildings across the road from where Tom Stewart had built the original farm buildings. This most likely had to do with water: With the buildings on the north side of the town road, Coombes could build a fenced lane from the barnyard to the pond, where the animals could find water during the long, hot days of summer when the windmill-operated pump was likely to fail due to lack of wind.

To the west of the new buildings, Coombes planted a string of black willow trees to serve as a windbreak. He likely hauled little black willows from Springwater Township east of Wild Rose, where the land is somewhat heavier and closer to water. Black willows like moist ground and do not grow naturally in this part of Rose Township. Weston and Charlotte carried pails of water all summer long to keep the trees alive and growing.

On January 16, 1913, John and Ina Coombes received a clear title to their farm, having satisfied the land contract held by D. R. Bowen. For the first time the John Coombes family owned land—even though it was far from being the best farm in the township of Rose.

By now the village of Wild Rose had progressed considerably. The upstairs of Patterson's store included a large hall with stage. The Wild Rose Times advertised a "Great Lecture Treat. At Patterson's Hall, February 19, the last number of the popular Lyceum course will be a lecture by that prince of platform entertainers, Charles Howard Plattenburg, 'The Cream of the Final Feast.'" Dances, lectures, and other programs were held in this substantial hall throughout the year. In that same newspaper, store owner F. M. Clark suggested that "[t]hese long winter evenings pass quickly and delightfully when you have some of our books and latest magazines."[7]

In 1913, 133 farm families lived in Rose Township.[8] Some were quite prosperous for the day, enough so that they gave their farms names. C. J. Olson called his 260 acres Fairview Farm; Ward Staples christened his 150 acres Valley View Farm. M. Urban, who owned 225 acres about three miles north of the Coombes farm, named his place Oak Hill Farm. Owen Williams's 200 acres were called Lone Birch Farm. And E. Owens, who had but 120 acres, nonetheless advertised as a "Breeder in Purebred Percheron Horses and Shropshire Sheep."[9]

~~~~~~

My grandparents on both sides lived in Rose Township in 1913. My grandfather George Apps and his family, including my father, Herman, then fourteen, farmed 160 acres just to the west of the Coombes place in section 32. My grandfather William Witt and his family,

Plat map of
Rose Township

*ATLAS AND FARMERS'
DIRECTORY OF
WAUSHARA COUNTY,
WISCONSIN,
CIRCA 1914*

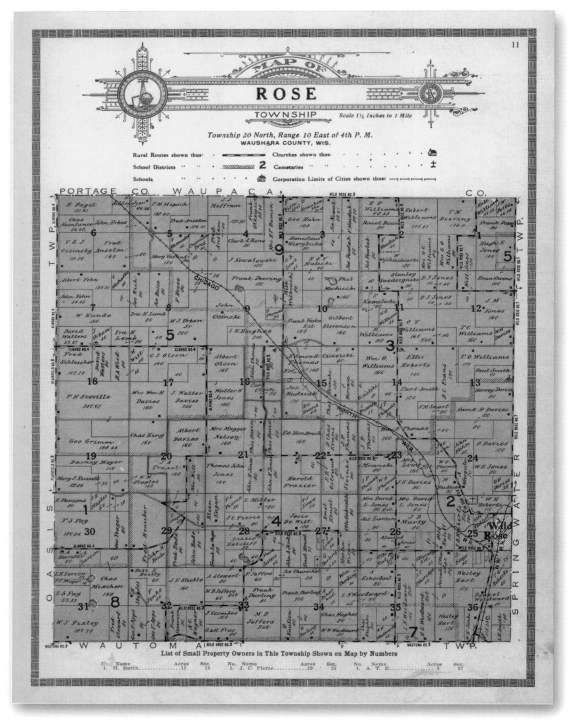

including my mother, Eleanor, who was eleven in 1913, lived on 120 acres northwest of the Coombes farm.[10]

Because the Coombes farm was only a couple miles from the farm where I grew up, I got to know the Coombes family well. Ina Coombes always said how happy she had been to return to the farm where she had been born in 1876.

"Not much of a farmer," Dad said about John Coombes. John never changed his way of farming, never bought a tractor, never planted improved seed corn or oat varieties. Never planted alfalfa. Never had electricity. Didn't drive a car. He continued farming oblivious to the reality that farming practices were changing dramatically during and right after World War II.

In 1946 John suffered a heart attack and died, leaving his widow, Ina, and son, Weston, to run the farm. Daughter Charlotte had moved to Wild Rose. They tried to follow in John's footsteps, each year planting the crops and each year harvesting less. Ina and Weston believed that the old way, John's way, was the best way to farm. The Coombeses had only six cows, mostly Guernseys, with one or two of unknown heritage. Dad once said, "Old John Coombes don't know a thing about cow feedin'. That's why his skinny cows never gave more'n a cup or two of milk. Except right after they were fresh and then the calves sucked up most of that. Far as I can see, Weston takes after his old man."

Ina and Weston enjoyed their farm life—and a simple life it was. Weston drove a leather-topped buggy pulled by a team of workhorses to town for provisions and to the neighbors for visiting. Where else was there to go?

Weston Coombes often worked for my dad, especially in the winter when there was wood to cut. I remember driving Weston home one frigid December day when I was in high school. I always felt the same way when I drove into the Coombes farmstead: depressed. The little gambrel-roofed barn and two-story granary had been built in the early 1900s and had never been painted. The barn had suffered through one too many windstorms and leaned toward the south.

John Coombes had fashioned some logs he'd cut in the woods into a makeshift little pig house. Now, years later, one end of it sagged toward the west, where the foundation logs had rotted. The roof had once been covered with tar paper, but the wind had torn most of it off. A tangled woven-wire lane led west from the pigpen, over a hill.

Since there was no machine shed on the property, Weston's machinery, all horse drawn, stood where he had unhitched the team when he last finished work. A rusty McCormick mower stood under some apple trees, and next to it the one-row cultivator lay tipped on its side. Nearby stood the steel-wheeled wagon. Various other machinery was scattered around the farmyard, leaving an overall impression of neglect and poor management.

Whenever I gave Weston a ride home, he invited me in for a cup of coffee. I usually declined, but we had just spent the day cutting wood behind our house until dark, wallowing around in deep snow, and I decided that a hot cup of coffee would taste good. We entered through the kitchen door, a common main entrance for farm homes in those days. I pulled off my boots and stood them by the door, took off my winter coat and hung it on a peg nearby. The Coombes house had been built the same time as the other buildings and was the same cold shade of gray. The house had never been finished. All that separated the kitchen from zero-degree weather and waist-deep snow were two-by-fours and well-weathered pine siding. I could see right through the wall in places. Here and there someone had nailed dismantled cardboard boxes to the bare two-by-fours—the house's only insulation. The house had no brick chimney. A metal stovepipe pushed up through the roof, extending a few feet above the ridge line. That stovepipe became dangerously hot on cold days requiring a blazing fire.

On the center of the bare wood kitchen table stood a kerosene lamp. The chimney on the lamp was absolutely spotless; the place may have been run down, but Ina Coombes liked things clean and neat inside her house. The lamp's yellow light cast an eerie shadow on the bare rafters. I could see frost on them, like the frost that would gather on the rafters of our haymow from the warm, moist breath of cows below; here the moisture came from Ina and Weston and the ever-present teakettle on the back of the cookstove. There was no plaster on the walls or the ceiling, and no insulation anywhere, common for houses built around the turn of the twentieth century.

A simple kitchen sink was attached to the wall beside the door leading outside, with a pipe attached to the bottom that stuck out through the outside wall. Whatever was in the sink spilled out into the snow, where it promptly froze into a grotesque little multicolored mound.

"Come in, come in," Ina said from where her rocking chair sat by the stove. "Come on over by the fire. Warm up. Sure a cold one today. I swear the thermometer ain't budged the entire day. Another night like the last one and we'll be buyin' new thermometers."

At seventy-four, Ina Coombes was a wrinkled, slightly stooped old woman who wore her white hair pulled back and rolled into a tight bun. She was tiny, not much taller than five feet. Slim and frail, she was not at all like most of the neighborhood women, who were husky and wide-shouldered. Of course, some of the physical differences between Ina and the neighbor women were likely due to ethnic background. The neighborhood had been settled by Germans,

Winter sunset

Welsh, Norwegians, and Poles, except for the Coombeses and a few other English neighbors. They were indeed English, and proud of it.

"All that red stuff in the thermometer will be froze into a little pile on the ground," she laughed quietly. "Get over here by the stove. You must be froze, workin' out in the woods all day."

What Ina lacked in physical size, she made up for in spirit. Ina had plenty of that. You could see it in her gray eyes that sparkled when she talked; you could hear it in her low voice that always communicated her interest, her deep caring. She had a keen sense of humor and could tell a good story with the best of them.

"Sit down, rest," Ina said. She got up from her chair and slowly walked to the cookstove. "You must be tired from being out in the cold."

I nodded, eyeing the coffeepot she was sliding across the stove. I pulled around a straight-backed chair from the table and sat down. Weston sat in an old stuffed chair that seemed to have a permanent place near the oven door. He never said much, no matter what the occasion, and this was no exception. He sat there, staring at the old wood range with watery eyes. His week-old black whiskers were well peppered with gray. As long as I'd known him I hadn't seen many changes, except for the gray whiskers.

Ina poured three cups of coffee from the sooty pot, thick, black, and hot. From somewhere on the counter, three large white cookies appeared. "Here you are," she offered. "This'll warm your innards. Help yourself to a cookie, too."

We sat sipping coffee, not saying much of anything. I noticed Weston yawning. A few minutes later his head dropped back and he was fast asleep.

"Gonna be a long, cold winter," Ina said. "Like those when I was a little girl." Ina liked recalling the stories she had heard from her folks when they lived on the farm.

"Was it colder then?" I asked.

"Colder? This ain't nothin'. I remember when I was ten years old. We went six weeks without the thermometer ever crawlin' above zero. Some mornings when I got up, the water pail, one just like that one over there, was froze solid. From the bottom to the top. My ma'd put it right on the hottest part of the stove, and it was still an hour before there was enough water for a decent drink."

In a repeated stories she'd heard from her parents about the Menominee Indians coming through Skunk's Hollow each spring on their way to the trading post in Berlin, thirty miles to the east. There the Indians traded hides trapped the previous winter for supplies such as salt and sugar. The younger children and the older women rode on travois tied to the sides of the

Intricate patterns on pond ice

horses. The Indians camped near the Stewarts' pond as they rested on their journey to the Fox River trading post. Their campfires sent spirals of oak smoke skyward.

"One of 'em could talk pretty fair English," Ina said. "The others probably could talk it, too, but seemed this one fella did most of the talkin'. Sometimes he and a couple of younger men would come up to the house and ask for sugar or salt, and they'd sit here by the stove and talk. Pa told me all about it.

"Some of the children in the neighborhood were frightened of the Indians," Ina said, "but there was nothing to be scared of. Pa said we never had any trouble with 'em; we didn't bother them, they didn't trouble us."

Ina located a metal pail in the corner of the kitchen. I watched her as she shuffled over to the pail and brought it to where we were sitting at the kitchen table. She reached in, pulled out an arrowhead, and handed it to me. I turned it over in my fingers, noticing how carefully it had been formed. The bucket was heaped with Indian points and arrowheads. "John found these plowing the field near the pond," she explained. Some of the arrowheads were copper, corroded to a rich, dark green. But most were stone, carefully shaped and chipped so the edges were sharp enough to penetrate the skin of a wild animal. There was a stone ax head in the pail, with two grooves chipped into its sides to allow the stone to be fastened with rawhide to a handle. I hefted the stone ax head, comparing it in my memory to the steel ax I had been using all day. The two ax heads seemed to be about the same weight.

With Weston dozing next to the woodstove and the teakettle sending a trickle of steam toward the bare ceiling, Ina Coombes continued telling stories of her growing-up years in the area. Although from my perspective she had next to nothing in the way of material possessions, her stories told of earlier times when she had even less, when the Stewarts were barely able to find enough to eat and making it through the winter was an annual challenge.

She told her stories not to evoke pity, but to share the facts of her childhood and to express how blessed she felt with what she had now. She wanted me to understand that there are things in life far more important than material possessions—good friends and neighbors, an opportunity to live on your own land, and reasonably good health. She had these, and she was pleased, even optimistic. As I have gotten older, I have increasingly appreciated the lessons I learned from this woman born on the very acres that are now mine.

One below-zero winter night in 1959, neighbors on the Wild Rose telephone exchange heard a general ring, five or six short rings that meant an emergency. People rushed to their telephones.

"The Coombes house is on fire! The Coombes house is on fire!" the operator shouted. In the 1950s village fire trucks would not travel into the countryside to fight fires. The fire departments were supported by village taxpayers, and that's who they served, no matter what the need in the country. Neighbors from all over the community rushed to the Coombes farm, but it was too late. Flames were leaping from the roof. There was no chance of saving the old gray house.

The Coombeses' pump house also caught fire, but neighbors threw water on it and saved the little gray building. The flames spared the granary and the barn to the north. Ina and Weston lost everything. Their furniture, clothing, keepsakes from a lifetime, Indian arrowheads—all gone. All that was left was a pile of ashes smoldering in the cellar and the twisted remains of the woodstove and stovepipe, the apparent cause of the fire. The trees in the willow windbreak west of the old house were singed, but they would survive.

After the disaster, Ina and Weston Coombes moved to Wild Rose to live with Weston's sister, Charlotte. For the first time in more than a hundred years, no one would live on the land that Tom Stewart had homesteaded in 1867.

PART II

Roshara

An abandoned town road cuts through the farm from east to west.

Chapter 8

◇◇◇◇◇◇◇◇◇◇◇◇◇◇◇◇◇◇◇◇

Lay of the Land

"The woods are lovely, dark and deep,
But I have promises to keep,
and miles to go before I sleep."
Robert Frost

When facing something new, Dad always said, check the lay of the land. In other words, find out as much as you can about what you are considering. After my brothers' and my purchase of the old Coombes place from my dad, I set out to literally check the lay of the land, to walk its acres, climb its hills, and check its boundaries—to look at the trees, grasses, and wildflowers, and the remnants of its history.

In the two years that my dad owned the land, the family had done little with it. We hunted there, and hiked to the pond on occasion, but little else. When my brothers, Donald and Darrel, and I bought the land from our father for one dollar in 1966, the three of us owned it together, with no legal division of the property. My brothers agreed I could have the buildings— at that time the barn, granary, and pump house had been taken off the tax rolls as worthless.

On a sunny October day in 1966, I set out on a hike to the west of the old buildings, past the massive black willow trees that form a windbreak for the farmstead. Branches thrust this way and that, as willow trees will do. The shaggy limbs had not yet dropped their leaves. The Coombes family had planted these trees as saplings. Now some of the grayish, deeply furrowed trunks were three or more feet across.

I walked across a two-acre field to a rather steep hill that dipped down to the pond. The oaks in the woods to the north were in full fall splendor, their leaves a riot of browns, reds,

Fall brings a collage of color to Roshara.

and tans shouting for attention. The rich smell of autumn, of dead grass and fallen oak leaves, hung in the air.

The hill was deeply cut with gullies caused by heavy rains. (The Coombes family had put a stop to the washing when they planted black willow trees on the hill in 1911, at the same time they planted the willow windbreak west of the buildings.) Sandy soil, as all the farmers who've owned this land know, is extremely fragile. Wind picks it up and moves it, and heavy rains rip gullies in its surface when the grade is steep.

I followed the remnants of a woven wire fence along the farm's northern boundary to the pond in the valley. The bright yellow of maples and aspen trees that ring the valley provided a stark contrast to the clear blue sky. Giant cottonwoods, three feet in diameter and more than sixty feet tall, grew on the edge of the pond. Their yellow leaves shook nervously as a slight breeze from the west washed across the pond's surface. It was easy to see that this unnamed pond was much larger at one time, as no trees grew where the water level had once been. More than a hundred feet of dry land stretched from the present water line to the level the pond had once reached. Gazing into the water, I saw minnows swimming and noticed where muskrats had burrowed into the pond's bank. I scared a green frog from its perch on a lily pad. Deer tracks had punched into the mud near the water; a deer had come for a drink earlier this day. And the handlike paw print of a raccoon showed it had been at the pond in search of breakfast. The smells of fall near water are pungent with dead and dying vegetation preparing for the long rest of winter.

Oak leaves add to the panorama.

Walking around the pond to the south, I saw more huge gullies cut in a steep side hill. Oak, aspen, and birch trees grew in the gullies, some of which were so deep you could hide a small building in them.

I climbed the hill west of the pond, still following the farm's north boundary. I walked among gigantic oak trees; their growth testified to the extra moisture and richer soil near the pond. Their leaves, some past full color, were just beginning to fall. I found John Coombes's wire fence nailed to trees here and there in the woods, some of the rusty wire torn loose by falling branches and heavy snows. The fence defined the farm's boundary and kept the Coombes cattle from roaming into the big woods to the north. In several places a tree had grown around the wires, which stuck out on either side of the trunk like thin, rusty handles. According to Dad, this grove of oak and aspen trees had once been a potato patch; he remembered helping John Coombes with the harvest some twenty or more years ago.

As I continued my journey west, the elevation continued to increase. At the northwest corner of the property, I could see the top of Mt. Morris, one of the tallest hills in Waushara County, about eight miles to the east.

Now I turned south, picking my way along the western boundary of the farm, along another fencerow with rusty wire and broken fence posts. A few hundred yards beyond the boundary line I spotted the foundation of what had been the Stickles farm (circa 1905). Stickles had owned the 160-acre quarter section north of my place. I did not know the present owners. I could make out the fieldstone walls of the barn—all that remained—and the foundation where the house once stood. The walking trail that begins at my farmstead and goes straight west had once been a town road that connected the Stickles farm with the rest of the world.

The remnants of a barbwire fence mark the northern boundary of the farm.
Oak trees have grown around the wire that was nailed to them.

I hiked along the western boundary, across a field of maybe five acres, once farmed but now abandoned. Here and there grew jack pine trees, which are native to the area, and Scotch pine, which are not. Christmas tree growers introduced Scotch pine to the area several years ago, and the pine seeds had spread widely.

I found hazelnut bushes, some hanging with ripe hazelnuts in their chocolate brown covers, and evergreen juniper bushes. Both hazelnut and juniper are natives.

At the southern boundary I turned east and walked first through a small grove of black and bur oak trees and then through a scattering of black cherry trees, jack pine, more Scotch pine, and another row of black willow planted as a windbreak. I emerged on a large, open field, twenty acres or more, that had once been a cornfield. It hadn't been plowed for several years, and I saw a scattering of Scotch and jack pine and even a few box elder trees that had self-seeded. The field was a garden of wildflowers. I found blue spiderwort and the small red flowers of sheep sorrel. Both grow well on acid, sandy soils. Some alternative medicine advocates claim that a tea made from sheep sorrel is antidiarrheal, anti-inflammatory, and antioxidant. Native people often referred to sheep sorrel as sour week or sour grass.

Patches of hawkweed were everywhere, some yellow, some orange. Black-eyed Susan grew here and there, now a couple months past its peak flowering time. Some botanists consider this beautiful and tough little flower, which will grow in the most difficult of situations, the most common of all wildflowers.

I spotted several stalks of common mullein growing in the field. Mullein is an impressive wildflower; some stalks will grow as high as five or six feet, even on sandy soil. Mullein is biennial, which means it lives two years. The first year it produces a rosette of yellow flowers; the second it sends up its tall stalk, which produces seeds. It's known as a pioneer plant, as it is one of the first to grow after soil has been disturbed. Generally classified as

Black-eyed Susans

an herb, mullein is not native to the United States; early European settlers brought the plant with them because of its medicinal qualities. Pioneers made a tea from the leaves to treat colds and used the flowers and roots to soothe ailments from earaches to coughs. Sometimes the leaves were applied to skin to sooth sunburn. Dad always called it Indian tobacco; the big, velvety leaves resemble tobacco leaves, and some claim that when smoked they provide a respiratory stimulant.

Goldenrods grew everywhere in my wildflower field, many in their full fall yellow finery. They grow in patches, mostly in hollows where the soil is a little richer and holds a bit more moisture. We had goldenrods on the home farm as well, and in the winter, before we set off for a day of ice fishing, we stuffed our pockets with goldenrod galls, little balls that grow on the goldenrod stem. Slicing open the gall with a jackknife, we'd find a little grub nestled there, insulated from the cold of winter. Bluegills, perch, and other panfish savored this tasty bait.

At one end of the field I found a patch of common milkweeds, their big, brown pods about to burst and release hundreds of seeds to fly away on the little gossamer parachutes attached to each. Without milkweeds we'd have few Monarch butterflies, as this plant is one of their primary food sources. The milky sap inside the milkweed's leaves and stem contains toxic cardiac glycosides. When the Monarch caterpillar eats the milkweed leaves, the glycosides

Ripe milkweed pods await a strong wind to distribute their seeds.

remain in its body, making the caterpillar poisonous to predators. (The adult butterfly continues to have glycosides in its body, making it poisonous to predators as well.) As I walked among the milkweeds, I remembered that during World War II my fellow country school students and I collected milkweed pods by the sackful and sent them away to become stuffing for life jackets worn by sailors and airmen.

I ambled across the big open field, thinking about Weston Coombes with his team of horses plowing, discing, and planting these acres, hoping for a good harvest but taking what he would get from this sandy soil.

The eastern edge of this field drops off quickly in a long, steep hill covered with Scotch and jack pine and a large patch of big bluestem grass. At the bottom of this hill, I pictured how these long valleys became the glacial streams that carried excess meltwater to the south and east, draining the area and forming the hills and valleys. I pondered the huge boulders scattered on our hilltops, wondered about their sources and how many thousands of miles they traveled embedded in a wall of ice before being left behind as the glacier receded.

At the top of another long, sandy hill, so barren that no grass grew there, I found only mosses and lichens. Along the top edge of the hill grew a north-south row of white pines forming another windbreak. The gentle breeze rustled the soft needles of these native trees, which grow in much of central and northern Wisconsin. Later I learned from Dad that John Coombes planted these pines during the 1930s, when drought plagued much of the country, including central Wisconsin. White pines grow quickly on sandy soil, and the trees blocked the dry winds that incessantly tore at the land, lifting the soil in huge dusty clouds and taking the fertility with it. As I walked along the rows of pines I saw huge mounds of soil piled against their trunks, evidence that the trees had served well in stopping the erosion.

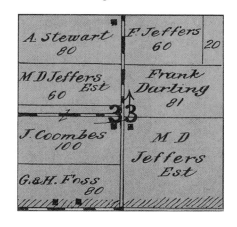

The circa 1914 Rose Township plat map shows the locations of the original farm buildings.

ATLAS AND FARMERS' DIRECTORY OF WAUSHARA COUNTY, WISCONSIN, CIRCA 1914

On the other side of the windbreak was another field of seven or eight acres where corn had once been planted. I found remnants of decaying cornstalks and saw where the plowman had left his mark with dead furrows and back furrows, the depressions and humps formed when the plow piles two furrows on top of each other. These furrows cut across the length of the field, according to how the plowman made them with his one-bottom walking plow pulled by a team of draft horses. I thought again of Weston Coombes, walking behind his plow, one foot in the furrow, the horses' reins draped across his shoulders, his hands gripping the handles of the plow. The sandy soil must have turned readily with no stones in the path of the plow, making the work relatively easy—if plowing with a one-bottom plow can ever be called easy.

Soon I was on 15th Road, still a gravel road in 1966 just as it had been in 1852 or 1853, when the first trail plunged through this area along the section lines made by land surveyors. In a little field immediately south of the driveway into our farm, I looked for remnants of where Tom Stewart built the first farmstead in 1867. The buildings still appear on a map in the township's circa 1914 plat book. Now all I could see was a flat area on top of a little rise, likely the place where the first cabin and barn had stood.

Hills and valleys, gullies and rusty wire fence, wildflowers and grasses, white pines and black oaks, remnants of cornfields, memories of cow pastures, high ground and pond—all are a part of the lay of the land at this old farm. All speak of its history.

Pump house boards scorched in the 1959 fire remain charred to this day.

Chapter 9

<small>◇◇◇◇◇◇◇◇◇◇◇◇◇◇◇◇◇◇◇◇◇</small>

Gray Buildings

"The cabin had not been built for summer comfort or view. It had no real-estate value."
SIGURD OLSON

Having completed my survey of my new land that October day in 1966, I turned my attention to the old, gray buildings. What stories would the remnants of the house and these decrepit old farm buildings reveal?

To the south of the barn, granary, and pump house, I saw the remnants of a barbwire fence with crooked posts, rusting wire, and a corner post braced with diagonal wooden poles. The fence surrounded a small field that Weston Coombes had used to pasture his small herd of Guernsey cows and the team of skinny horses that powered his rusty farm equipment.

The pump house overlooked another fenced field, once the Coombes barnyard. A few box elder trees lined the barnyard fence, volunteers that sprouted and grew rapidly after the Coombes family moved away. The pump house sheltered the pump and well that provided water for the farm. The south side of the pump house's pine siding was scorched and burned, a reminder of the fire that destroyed the farmhouse a few years earlier. A windmill once straddled the pump house. Perched at the top of the windmill tower, twenty or more feet up, had been a big metal wheel with fans designed to catch the slightest breeze. The wind would spin the wheel, which moved a pump rod up and down. The pump rod moved within a two-inch pipe that was pounded into the ground sixty-plus feet down to water. As the rod went up and down, a valve at the end opened and closed, moving water up the pipe and then

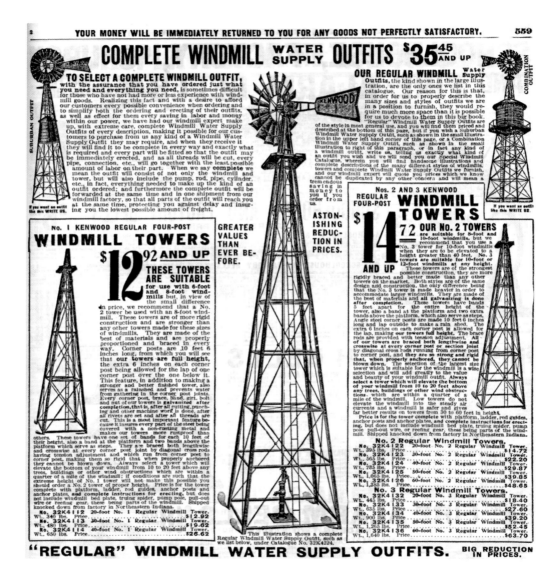

The Coombes family used a windmill like this one to pump water.

SEARS, ROEBUCK CATALOG, 1908, FROM THE AUTHOR'S COLLECTION

through another iron pipe to a water tank in the barnyard. In the roof was a trapdoor-type opening so that pump rods from the well could be pulled if the pump required repair.

In 1908 Sears, Roebuck and Company offered a complete windmill outfit consisting of a six-foot windmill fan, twenty-foot windmill tower, lift pump, pump rods, and "instructions for erecting the windmill and tower" for $35.45. It was a simple, inexpensive, and nearly foolproof way of pumping water. But a windmill required wind, and that could be a problem. During the hot, dry days of summer—when cattle and other livestock demanded the most water—the wind often didn't blow and the windmill wheel didn't turn. This is likely the reason that John Coombes fenced a lane to the pond: so his livestock would always have access to water.

The pump house once had three little windows on the south side, two on the north side, and two on the east end. As I walked around the little outbuilding I saw that all were broken. Only dark holes remained on walls that were never painted, like sunken eyes in grayish skin. The rickety door at the west end of the building stood ajar, so critters of every description— red squirrels, woodchucks, field mice, chipmunks, bats, and barn swallows—moved freely in and out of the building. The roof was wood shake shingles, the old red cedar kind that last a lifetime provided the wind doesn't tear them lose. But the wind had taken many of them, and sunlight shone through the roof on this bright autumn day. Shafts of light caught the dust in the air and made splotches of color on the brown dirt floor.

I stepped back outside and found the foundation of the farmhouse, scarcely visible in the tall grass, a hundred feet west of the pump house. The cellar hole and a few stones lined up in a rectangle define where the house once stood. I could still see the rusty metal of the old woodstove in the cellar hole, partially covered with ashes and with weeds and grass that had mostly overgrown the site.

A bit farther north stood a two-story granary with a chicken house lean-to. The one-story lean-to had three little windows, all broken. A faded gray door stuck fast when I tried to pull it open. The granary had two broken windows and a big gray entry door on the southeast corner, fastened with a wooden latch. I quickly discovered that Weston Coombes had housed his team of horses inside the granary. Where once had been grain bins now were horse stalls and dried piles of horse manure. The manger was half full of moldy timothy hay. Harnesses, a leather halter, and bridle with bit hung on the granary wall, the leather dried and mildewed. Barn swallow nests were tucked up against the ceiling joists; long skeins of cobwebs brushed my face. The smells of old manure and dusty hay engulfed me.

Just inside the granary door I crawled up a rickety ladder, nothing more than a series of narrow wooden strips nailed between two-by-four studs. In the dingy, dusty upstairs, I saw where Weston had dried seed corn and stored extra harnesses. Cobwebs hung from the ceiling. Bat dung lay everywhere on the floor; bats had taken over the upstairs of the granary and made it their home.

I climbed back down and walked around the back side of the granary. A wagon shed, with double doors on each side, had been added to the north side of the building, and a narrow, slatted corncrib was attached to the side of the wagon shed. This was clearly a multipurpose building built to store oats, rye, and wheat; house chickens; dry seed corn; house a buggy; and store cob corn—all under one roof, and handy for doing chores.

Just to the north of the corncrib stood a small gambrel-roofed barn. At first glance the barn appeared substantial, clearly the tallest and largest building of the three-building cluster. But looking closely, I quickly saw that the barn had serious structural problems. The bottom of the building up to where the roofline began was leaning severely to the south. The top part of the barn leaned to the north. Weston Coombes had placed a row of a half dozen eight-foot, six-inch-diameter cedar posts at an angle along the south side of the barn to brace the building so it wouldn't fall on the wagon shed and granary. Now it was clear why Weston kept his horses in the granary—he was afraid the barn would tip over. It appeared as though it might happen any time—a stiff windstorm or heavy snow would do the job.

I carefully pulled open a barn door and entered—it seemed safe for the moment. I stood still and listened and looked. Although I had a somewhat eerie feeling, I heard no creaking and saw no movement. A row of stanchions that once confined the Coombes cattle stood rusty and abandoned, with manure gutters behind them and feed mangers in front, still filled with musty hay.

Using a wooden ladder fastened to the barn wall, I climbed to the haymow. There I found a few feet of moldy hay, a broken hay fork rope, and a hay fork hanging from its track high up in the peak. Small square windows on each end of the barn allowed pigeons, bats, swallows, and other flying creatures easy access. I spotted a barn swallow nest high up in the rafters. A swallow on the nest flew out the window when she saw me. The slight breeze that fall afternoon sifted around the corners of the old, dying barn, making sounds of mourning. The smell of old, forgotten days was everywhere.

Outside again, I found the Coombes outhouse, a two-holer of the same never-painted

Black willow trees planted by John Coombes in 1912 continue to serve as a windbreak for the farm buildings.

gray as the other farm buildings, tucked under the black willows. I inspected the row of old black willow trees that for decades has protected the farm buildings from the northwest winds and the summer storms that can be fierce in this part of Wisconsin. Even with the windbreak for shelter, the old barn had become a victim of the elements. Abandoned and forgotten, in many ways the buildings were symbols of the farm itself. Later we learned that the buildings had been declared worthless by a tax assessor and taken off the tax rolls.

Some of Dad's friends asked why he had purchased this seemingly worthless, abandoned place, with its unpredictable harvests and ramshackle buildings. He just smiled and said he wanted some land for his boys. Now, some forty years later, I can't thank him enough for seeing something more in this place than tax-delinquent acres and worthless buildings.

Artifacts left in the pump house from an earlier day, when farmers saved everything, including old nails

Chapter 10

Pump House

"John Coombes, Wild Rose, Wis. N.W. Bag.
In case of loss notify Blue Valley Creamery Company."

BRASS PLATE ON FIVE-GALLON CREAM CAN

Every building has a story. The old pump house on my farm is no exception. John Coombes made the building twelve feet wide, sixteen feet long, and twelve feet tall at the peak of its gable roof. The side walls are eight feet high. Whether he was aware of it or not, Coombes was building for the future when he constructed the building on a poured concrete wall. Many farmers, especially in the poorer sections of the Upper Midwest, found some big fieldstones and piled them under the corners of a building for support. That had to be good enough.

It is not difficult to picture John and his son, Weston, mixing mud (as preparing concrete was called in those days). So many shovels full of Portland cement, so many shovels full of screened sand—the wood-frame screen was tucked up under the roof, where it remains today. Pour in some water from the newly dug well and mix it with a hoe until it turns a dark gray and pours—but just barely.

Before they mixed the concrete, they made forms from two-inch planks that they braced with two-by-four lumber. The forms would hold the wet concrete in place until it dried and became hard. All this took some thinking and planning, for the pump house is not on level ground. On the west side of the building the concrete foundation is only six inches or so high; on the east side it is three feet high. Perhaps John Coombes had the savvy to plan all of this so the building would be straight with the world—a phrase country people used when describing how new buildings must point straight north and south, or east and west. The pump house, situated east and west, was built of ten-inch pine boards nailed to the full-cut two-by-four studs.

On one of my first inspections of the building, I found, tucked under the eaves near the roof, a brass stencil of the name Tom Stewart—no doubt the stencil Tom had used during the Civil War to mark his gear. That simple brass marking plate, the only artifact I have that ties Tom directly to the Civil War, set me on a research adventure that lasted several years. In addition to housing the well, the little pump house became a collecting place for farm paraphernalia. The building was a veritable farm museum, a collection of tools from the early 1900s to the mid-1950s. The full inventory of what I unearthed there follows; I have not disturbed the artifacts, although I have spent many hours pondering the stories they tell me about this old farm that I now own.

- **Five-gallon cream can with brass tag: "John Coombes, Wild Rose, Wis. N.W. Bag. In case of loss notify Blue Valley Creamery Company."** John Coombes, along with his neighbors, separated the cream from the milk his cows gave and shipped the cream by rail to Milwaukee on the Chicago Northwestern Railroad. He fed the skim milk that remained to his hogs. In those days, most people drank whole milk and wouldn't think of drinking skim.
- **Two pieces of oak wood, two and a quarter inches by two and a quarter inches, six feet long. Six drag teeth pounded through each.** Farmers used a drag to smooth the soil after it was plowed and disced. The one John Coombes used was homemade, and these were the spare parts.
- **Barbwire without barbs, but with metal pointers.** This roll of barbwire is some of the earliest barbwire made. John Coombes had likely replaced this old wire with a more modern version. The points of this old wire are shaped like little triangles and are not nearly as treacherous as the modern versions.
- **Ten gallon milk can, rusty.** Once cheese factories opened in the area, John Coombes would have a milk truck pick up ten-gallon cans of his whole milk each day and haul the milk to the Wild Rose Cheese Factory, where it was made into cheese. Whey, a byproduct of the cheesemaking process, was returned to the farmer, who fed it to his pigs.
- **Three huge oak bobsled runners, turned up in front.** Many farmers transferred their wagon box to the bobsled when the first snows began accumulating in late fall. John Coombes was probably intent on building a new bobsled, as these wooden runners had never been used. I never found the fourth one needed to construct a complete bobsled.
- **Buggy tongue.** The Coombes family traveled to town and throughout the neighborhood by

horse and buggy. The tongue separates the horses and steers the buggy when the driver uses the reins to turn in one direction or another.

+ **Two sets of single wooden horse shafts for a buggy, for use when one horse pulled a buggy or cart.** These long wooden poles would be fastened at one end to the buggy and wide enough apart so a horse could fit between them.
+ **Double harpoon hay fork with metal pulley** (available in the 1908 Sears, Roebuck catalog for eighty-six cents).

A harpoon-type hayfork was once used to lift loose hay into the barn.

+ **Wooden hay fork block, for hay rope** (forty-five cents each in 1908).
+ **Four horseshoes.**
+ **Wooden whiffletree** (sometimes called whippletree). Each horse on the team was hitched to a wooden whiffletree; the whiffletrees were in turn fastened to another wooden piece, usually oak, making a doubletree.
+ **Two doubletrees:** a light metal one for a buggy, a heavier wooden one for farm implements.
+ **Chain end of a harness tug;** connected the horse's harness to the whiffletree.
+ **Wooden neckyoke;** connected the horse's collar to the implement's tongue (a wooden shaft).
+ **Wooden hame;** slightly curved piece of wood or metal that connected the horse harness trace or tug to the horse collar.
+ **Old-fashioned fly sprayer,** used to keep flies off of animals while they were being milked.
+ **Scythe handle.**
+ **Scythe blade.**
+ **Two harness snaps;** variously used on horse harnesses to fasten leather pieces together.
+ **Two one-pound General Foods Wonder Coffee cans full of rusty nails.**
+ **One-pound Breakfast Cup Coffee can full of rusty nails.**
+ **La Palina Deluxe cigar box.**
+ **Handle from a potato planter,** wrapped with cloth; from a one-person hand-operated potato planter that plants one potato seed at a time.
+ **Pieces of harness leather.**

(continued on following page)

- **Plates from a horse-drawn corn planter;** these metal plates regulated how far apart the corn kernels were planted in a row.
- **Pump with handle;** star on front and "Seneca Falls" inscription. Seneca Falls, New York, was the location of a major water pump manufacturer.
- **Orange Crush soda bottle.**
- **Four links from a link chain,** like those used on various farm implements, such as a grain binder.
- **Screen for screening sand for concrete making.**
- **Small steel clevis,** a U-shaped metal device with a hole in each end through which a pin or bolt could be pushed.
- **Pump jack for gasoline engine.**
- **Length of rusty metal stovepipe.**
- **Workbench across front of building with window looking out toward road.**

Our old pump house, built in 1912, stands as it did the day it was completed. The only changes we have made are adding a new roof and some paint on its tired, gray boards. It is the only original building on the farm that remains essentially untouched from the day John Coombes built it.

Chapter 11

Old Barn

"That barn'll fall down any minute—it's just hanging there now."
Darrel Apps

Our farmstead in 1966, including granary with chicken house lean-to, gambrel roof barn in back, and pump house on the right. The farmhouse, originally located between the granary and the fence, burned down in 1959. Daughter Susan is in the foreground.

PHOTO FROM THE AUTHOR'S COLLECTION

As we began figuring out how to make this farm part of our lives, practical matters became a priority. My wife, Ruth, and I discussed what we might do with the place. Living here full time was out of the question; we both had jobs in Madison. But we could spend weekends and vacation time at our new farm. My brothers were busy with jobs and families, too. Darrel was in graduate school in Madison and would soon move with his family to Kentucky; Donald owned a barbershop in Sheboygan, and he and his family would be happy with occasional camping trips to the farm.

One of Ruth's and my major concerns was the buildings—they were fifty-five years old and had been neglected for many years. The boards had never been painted; the roofs had deteriorated. Broken windows allowed the rain inside. One look at these old buildings and the practical answer was to tear them down—or perhaps invite the local volunteer fire department to come out and burn them as a practice exercise. But even in their decrepit condition, there was something distinctive about these old structures. Perhaps it was the history and stories associated with them. Maybe it was the inherent beauty of rough wood aged to silver.

Ruth and I quickly decided to save the granary and convert it into a cabin if possible. But the barn would have to go. And we'd have to act quickly; it was listing badly toward the south, with the granary in its path. Dad, Ruth, and I agreed that the barn had maybe another winter, maybe not even that long to stand.

"How do you tear down an old barn?" I asked an engineer friend in Madison.

"Hire a wrecking company," he answered.

"But I can't afford a wrecking company."

"Well, tearing down an old building is dangerous work, not something a teacher should tackle."

"I want to give it a try," I said quietly.

"Good luck," he said, shaking his head as he walked away.

In the fall of 1966 I was on leave from my teaching job at the University of Wisconsin, attending graduate school full time. The Vietnam War was accelerating. B-52 bombers had begun conducting raids on North Vietnam. Some of the fiercest fighting so far was taking place. Student unrest on college campuses increased. Tear gas filled the air on campus nearly every day. Students marched by the hundreds down State Street in Madison, their shouts of "Hell no, we won't go" piercing the air.

One warm day, far from the turmoil, Ruth and I stood looking at the old barn.

"How do I do this?" I wondered aloud. "How do I take down this old barn? Do I start at the top and work down, or start at the bottom and let the barn settle as I work? And what about the lean? How do I keep the barn from falling on the granary as I work?"

I quickly answered the question of where to start. I hate heights. Three steps up a stepladder and I am in trouble, and the barn was probably forty feet tall. Besides, it had a rotten roof. I'd have to start at the bottom. But how?

Ruth didn't have an answer, but she did suggest, "It sure would be nice if you saved the old barn boards. Nothing prettier than old barn boards." I agreed. Maybe we could use the old boards to repair the granary.

I borrowed a wrecking bar and a hammer and began work the following Saturday morning. Starting

An oak board taken from the barn

on the inside, in the corner farthest away from the granary, I tapped the first board with the hammer; the nails pulled through, leaving two rusty holes. When I pounded the other end of the board it splintered; the nails on that end cracked the dry board. That board broke, and so did the next one. Even being exceedingly careful, I managed to salvage only about one board in five.

The dust my pounding stirred up was almost unbearable. I removed a few more boards and then went outside to fill my lungs with clean air. It was time for more decisions. I had worked half a day and hadn't removed half the boards from the barn's north end—and there were far more boards on the barn's long sides. "At this rate, I'll be five years tearing down this blamed barn," I said to myself.

I gave up trying to save the boards; it was no use. I tried to kick them loose from the still-sturdy two-by-four studs. Some broke easily; others wouldn't budge when I hit them with my heavy army boot. I pounded the stubborn ones with the wrecking bar to jar them loose, breaking them into many pieces in the process.

Disappointed, I told Ruth and Dad about my morning's work. "Tell you what I'll do," Dad said. "I'll bring down the Farmall H this afternoon. Maybe we can pull the barn apart with that. You should pick up a burning permit, too, so you can burn the splintered wood. Won't have such a mess then."

Dad's tractor speeded the process considerably. I hooked a chain around the boards, climbed on the tractor, and started to pull. The chain snapped the boards loose from the studs. We built a fire and threw the splintered boards into the flames. The burning wood crackled and snapped, sending a plume of gray smoke skyward. If the barn had ever caught fire, all of the buildings would have burned, and fast. Just a few of the splintered boards made a roaring fire.

Still, as I watched the leaping flames, I wondered if we had made the right decision to tear down the old barn. Perhaps it could have been straightened and saved. The practical farm boy side of me said we were doing the right thing. But I still had some misgivings.

During the 1960s the United States saw a back-to-the-land movement, when many urban young people bought or rented a few acres, made a small garden, and tried to "live off the land." Many of these efforts failed when they discovered how hard this life is. You don't just sit around watching the sunrise and the sunset, read poetry under a shade tree, and discuss Emerson and Thoreau or Mao and Lenin all day. Living off the land, growing food and caring for animals, is hard work; ask any farmer and he or she will tell you.

I admit to having some romantic notions of rural living. But I grew up on a farm and knew the hard-work side of farm life as well. Yes, we watched the sunrise and the sunset. Yes, I found time to read many books on a variety of topics. But I also knew that if we were to eat and have a roof over our heads, we had to put the practical side of farming first. It's a lot easier to be romantic with a full belly and a roof that doesn't leak.

That afternoon we tore most of the boards loose from the bottom quarter of the barn. But we still hadn't answered a crucial question: How would we keep the barn from falling on the granary? "I'll have to think on that," Dad said as we finished up for the day. "It's getting too late to worry about it tonight."

When we returned the following weekend, the barn looked the same. It didn't appear to have moved and wasn't threatening the granary any more than before.

"Think I got it figured out," Dad said. "We'll pull the studs out from the north side; then the barn'll have to lean to the north. Once we got it leanin' north and moving away from the granary, the project'll be easy."

I hooked the heavy logging chain to the two-by-four studs, one by one, and Dad pulled them loose with the tractor. All that held the north end of the barn erect now was four four-by-four-inch posts holding up a beam under the haymow floor. The area under the haymow was empty except for the posts; we had already removed the board walls and the studs. The upper part of the barn seemed to be floating, but it did not move, despite considerable cracking and snapping as the upstairs support braces accepted heavier loads. After its long struggle with the elements, the old barn was refusing to surrender to two men and a tractor.

My brother Darrel and his wife, Marilyn, had stopped by to watch.

"Well, what're you gonna do now?" Darrel asked. "You can't go back under the barn and hook a chain to those skinny posts. That barn'll fall down any minute—it's just hanging there now."

"Do you have a better idea?" I asked.

"Nope," Darrel said.

I quickly hooked the chain to the first post and ran from under the barn. The Farmall spun its tires a half turn, and the post snapped with a loud bang and slid out from under the barn. The barn stood stalwart, not moving.

I ran in, carefully hooked the chain to the second post, and quickly retreated to safety. Again the post snapped, but the barn stood fast. Now only two posts held up the north end.

I repeated with post three, with similar results. Now the barn stood with but one skinny oak post holding up the north end.

"You can't go in there anymore," Marilyn said. "It'll come down any minute. See, it's swaying."

She was right. The snapping and cracking from the upstairs was growing louder.

"Let's just sit for a while and wait," Dad suggested. Dad was known for stopping and waiting when the outcome wasn't clear. This was surely one of those times.

We sat for fifteen minutes or so, watching the old barn in its death throes. It was a proud old structure, holding fast to its one thread of life.

"She's not comin' down as long as that post stands," Dad finally said.

I crept carefully under the barn, listening for a change in the sounds from upstairs. Underneath, the cracking from the protesting beams in the haymow was much louder. Perspiration ran down my back in a stream. I hooked the chain around the post and then hurried outside. My hands were shaking.

"Pull it loose," I yelled to Dad on the tractor.

The heavy tractor tires bit into the earth as the chain tightened and dug into the oak post. Then the post snapped loose, and the north end of the barn crashed to the ground with a great cloud of timothy hay dust mixed with spiderwebs and pigeon droppings.

We had solved one major problem. The barn would not fall on the granary. But it was a long way from being razed. The south end was still erect, though it was now leaning toward the north.

Later that afternoon, Ruth brought the children to watch. Dad and I now worked confidently as we took apart the south end of the structure, and before long the south end of the barn collapsed to the ground. When the dust settled, Sue, Steve, and Jeff came over to look at the strange barn with its roof on the ground.

"What's that noise?" Steve asked.

"I don't hear anything," I answered.

"Can't you hear it, Dad?"

This time I did. Little birds peeping. With a rush of terrible guilt, I realized I hadn't remembered to take the little swallows from their nests before pulling down the south end of the barn. Now they were buried in the wreckage. The swallow parents circled overhead; they too could hear the cries of their babies buried in the pile of twisted and splintered wood.

"Get them out, Dad!" Steve cried, tears running down his cheeks. Sue and Jeff were crying too, and looking at me as if I was the cruelest person in the world.

I chopped through the boards for more than a half hour, with no success. I couldn't find the baby swallows, and after fifteen or twenty minutes we couldn't hear them anymore. Perhaps they had suffocated in the dusty hay from the mow. Or perhaps a board had crushed them. The barn was down, but there was no happiness for the Apps family that night.

Chapter 12

Granary

"Sometimes hard to get horse smell out of an old building like this."
OLE KNUTSON

The cabin and pump house in fall

In the spring of 1967, with the barn mostly down, we turned our attention to the granary. I was back teaching at the university after a year's leave to complete a graduate degree, and I looked forward to spending more time at the farm—and figuring out where we could stay when we visited there with our children, then five, four, and three.

Wood salvaged from the old barn shows worm holes.

It was a quiet, cool day in late April 1967 when we arrived at the farm to spend a couple days planting trees and finish tearing down the old barn— what a contrast to what was going on in Madison. I was clearly living in two worlds: a university environment swirling with debate, protest, and marching, and the bucolic world of our farm, where the smell of freshly turned soil reminded me of other springs, where bluebirds were arriving to build nests and grass was beginning to turn green.

With the trees planted, Dad and I turned to salvaging what we could from the old barn. But the never-painted boards were dry and brittle, and we managed to save only a couple of the smaller timbers, which we used in the granary renovation.

Before we left for our return trip to Madison, Ruth and I carefully inspected the old granary. Earlier in the spring we had stopped at a local lumberyard that was selling A-frame cabins for "lake living." One model in particular caught our eye and seemed like a shelter that would fit in well at the farm. The building was twenty-four feet by thirty-two, and the package included all the lumber, precut, along with concrete piers and timbers for the base foundation. The main frame for the building was preassembled and ready to erect. The building included a loft, a front deck with benches, asphalt shingles, and a circular stairway to the loft. We discussed how we'd erect the new A-frame cabin just west of the black willow windbreak, away from the old farmstead, on a little hill that would allow us to see the pond to the west and open fields to the south.

Our dreams evaporated when the salesman at the lumberyard said, "You get all this for $3,000. Of course, the front deck, wood shingles, and stairway add up to another $700. We'd deliver the whole package for a hundred dollars. And, if you don't want to put it up yourself, you could probably find a carpenter to do it for three or four thousand."

My not-so-proficient mental calculating machine was adding things up. I had already reached about seventy-five hundred dollars when I looked at Ruth. She wasn't smiling.

"Do you realize," she said, "that after we spend all that money, all we'd have is a shell? No interior walls, no insulation, no wiring, no plumbing."

"Yes," I said, rather dejected.

We examined the granary with new purpose now that we knew we couldn't afford to build a cabin. Inside the old granary, we were once more reminded that Weston Coombes had housed his team of skinny horses there for two or three winters. With warmer temperatures we caught the pungent smell of horse manure mixed with the moldy and rotting timothy hay still in the makeshift mangers Weston had constructed for his team.

We measured the structure with my yardstick. It was fourteen by twenty feet. The chicken house lean-to was ten by fourteen feet.

"I think it's large enough," Ruth said, but without much enthusiasm. She brushed aside a big cobweb that dangled from the ceiling. "I suppose we could use the upstairs for sleeping— if we could ever get it clean enough."

"But look at the walls," I said. I showed Ruth where Weston's horses had eaten a two-by-four stud halfway through. Horses will do that sort of thing, not because they are hungry, more likely just bored and looking for something to do. I pointed out holes in the wall where hungry rats and mice had chewed their way into the granary in search of a meal.

All the windows were broken, the frames rotten beyond repair. The building's one door, on the southeast corner, was made of rough boards, now so warped the door wouldn't close completely. Boards were missing from the outside wall, exposing the two-by-four studs to the weather. The granary had a poured concrete floor, but someone or something had punched a huge hole through the floor. Broken pieces of concrete were scattered about.

Ruth and I crawled up the rickety ladder to the upstairs. We encountered discarded leather harnesses, stiff, cracked, and moldy. Brass buckles and short lengths of brittle leather. Three badly worn horse collars, all chewed by mice. Slats from the reel of a grain binder—the part of the binder that pushes the standing grain against the sickle so it is more easily cut. Several lengths of smooth wire strung between the rafters that Weston Coombes had used for drying seed corn over winter. Thick dust and dirty cobwebs everywhere.

Next we inspected the chicken house lean-to, attached to the west side of the granary. Here, too, the windows were broken and boards were missing from the walls. The chicken house had a dirt floor and wooden poles nailed across the north end of the structure for roosts—still covered with dried chicken manure. A few dilapidated nest boxes for the laying hens were attached to the east wall.

Steve and Jeff peek into the corncrib attached to the north side of the granary, 1968.

The tops of them were also coated with dried manure. Mouse holes were everywhere. Hungry mice regularly shared grain with Ina's small flock of chickens. The lingering smell of chicken manure mixed with the horse smell.

A quick tour of the dirty, dusty old building, with its leaking roof and battered siding, suggested it wasn't worth saving. But was the basic structure sound? Dad suggested he call his friend Ole, a retired carpenter from Wild Rose, and ask him to take a look at the building and give us his opinion.

Ole Knutson was born January 5, 1899, in Norway and came to the United States in 1903. He and his family lived a mile or so east of our farm, and he attended Chain O' Lake School, the same one I attended years later. When Ole started school he knew not one word of English, as his parents always spoke Norwegian at home. Ole had been a carpenter in Chicago for many years before returning home to retire.

I had taken a few days' vacation the next week. That Monday morning a green car pulled into the yard and a tall, broad-shouldered man in his late sixties and wearing dark-rimmed glasses stepped out into the bright sunshine. "Name's Ole Knutson," he said as he thrust out his big hand to shake mine. "Hear you're plannin' to make this old building into a cabin."

As we approached the granary, I told him we were thinking about it but needed to know if the building was worth saving. "Heard Coombes had horses in here," Ole said, sniffing. "Sometimes hard to get horse smell out of an old building like this. Good scrubbin' will sometimes do it. Adding some new lumber also helps take away the horse smell."

"That's good," Ruth said. "People have told us the place will always smell like a horse barn."

Ole surveyed the exterior of the granary. He unfolded his rule and measured the building's length and width and inspected the foundation. "When was this building built?" he asked.

"I believe it was 1912," I answered.

"Got to hand it to those carpenters; they built a good wall under this place. Lots of carpenters in those days set the sill on stones, or even on the ground. But you've got a concrete wall, and the sill doesn't seem rotten at all."

He climbed the makeshift ladder and looked around upstairs. I followed, watching closely. "Floor seems all right up here. 'Course, you'll need to insulate the roof and put some windows in to give you more light. And you'll need a new stairway. You'll kill yourself on this old ladder."

"What about the downstairs floor where the concrete is broken up?" I asked.

"That's easy. Just put another floor right over the top; the ceiling's high enough."

Back outside, Ole looked around and shook his head. "Here's your biggest problem," he said. "Siding is no good, too rotten to save. Never been painted, full of holes . . . you'll need new siding."

"Just a minute, Ole," I said. "Are you saying the granary is worth fixing?"

"Sure is; no question about that. I've seen new buildings that ain't built as well as this old granary. 'Course, you've got some work here, lots of it."

I was reluctant to ask the next question.

"Say, Ole, how about hiring you to help us?"

"Nope, not me. I can't work. Look at my hands—arthritis. I can barely hold a hammer anymore. Hands ache so I can't sleep. That's why I quit my carpenter job in Chicago— couldn't stand it with these bum hands."

"I don't know much about carpentry," I said. "Do you suppose you could tell me what to do?"

"That I can do, by golly. I'll make you a deal seein' as how you're kinda stuck and carpenters are hard to come by, especially in the summer. I'll help with the measurin' and tell you what to do every day; then I'll go back to town and you can work. How'd that be?"

I agreed with Ole's offer and shook his hand. Ruth was smiling—she knew that we needed all the help we could get. Now that we knew the granary was worth saving and we'd lined up a professional carpenter to help, it was time to go to work. Putting a new roof on the building was the first task. Cleaning out the inside of the building and scrubbing every square inch of the remaining wood came next.

Thunderstorms added a challenge to camping at the farm.

Chapter 13

◇◇◇◇◇◇◇◇◇◇◇◇◇◇◇◇◇◇◇◇◇◇

Cleanup

"I will not sleep in the same room with a mouse."
RUTH APPS

The first few summer vacations after we bought the farm we pitched an old umbrella tent under the shade of the big black willow trees that had served as a windbreak for the farmstead. The kids were little tykes at the time, enjoying every minute of their new camping experience.

We had added a new building to the farmstead that made camping possible, the first new building on the site since 1912. No matter that it was a two-holer outhouse, it was new, and it smelled new. An employee of the Wild Rose Lumberyard built it for us and hauled it out to the farm. The kids and I spent an afternoon painting it. By late afternoon, everything was brown— the outhouse, the grass around it, and of course the kids. All brown. Ruth was not especially happy and wondered how I had let the painting get so out of hand that even the faces of the kids were brown. I just smiled and reminded her that the outhouse was painted. She dropped the topic.

We lit our campsite with a Coleman gasoline lantern and cooked our meals on a Coleman gas stove. Mosquitoes menaced us some evenings, but camping was mostly a pleasant experience, with a few exceptions.

Our nearly daily afternoon treat after working to clean up the years of clutter accumulated in the Coombes yard was to go swimming. One sultry day in August 1968 I noticed a solid line of thunderstorms building in the western sky as we drove home from the Kusel Lake beach, a few miles east of Wild Rose.

Back at our campsite, I saw how quickly the clouds were moving and heard the deep growl of thunder. "We'll have sandwiches for supper," Ruth said. "Something we can put together in a hurry."

Jeff checks out the tent, an old, badly worn one we purchased for $27.50.
PHOTO FROM THE AUTHOR'S COLLECTION

By the time we finished our meal, the booming thunder was almost continuous and jagged slashes of lightning cut across the threatening sky. We quickly stowed our cooking gear, and I checked on the tent pegs and guy ropes to make sure everything was holding fast. The first drops of rain came down, huge drops that splattered on the driveway's dry ground. With everyone in the tent, I zipped the door shut. Raindrops fell faster, and a brisk wind shook the canvas.

Sitting on the floor in the tent, we not only heard the pounding rain and thunder, we felt the ground shake with each thunderclap. Inside the tent was total darkness, punctuated regularly by flashes of lightning as if someone were turning a light switch off and on. If the kids were frightened, they didn't show it. Ruth looked concerned. I know I was—mainly fearing the possibility of a tornado.

The black willow windbreak behind the tent was doing its job. The flimsy canvas shuddered only a few times as the wind gusted, but the deluge continued for nearly an hour. Then, as quickly as the storm started, it stopped. Out of the tent, I inspected for damage but saw none. All the cooking equipment was in good order. No downed tree limbs, no damage to the old granary.

In the east, a gigantic rainbow stretched from one horizon to the other—one of the largest I've ever seen. Soon, underneath it, another rainbow appeared.

"Dad," Susie said. "We want to climb the rainbow. Can you take us over there where it starts?" She was pointing to the southeast. "Over there" to the children must have seemed a few hundred yards away.

I muttered something about the rainbow being farther away than it appeared, but I doubt the kids believed me. They were now content splashing in the puddles left by the storm.

When I inspected the inside of the tent more carefully, I noticed that rainwater had seeped underneath and soaked a couple of the sleeping bags. We had been busy all week cleaning and scrubbing the inside of the granary in preparation for some carpentry work, and we had already put a new roof on the building, so I knew it was dry inside. "How about sleeping in the granary tonight?" I asked. "I know it's dry in there."

The kids thought it was a great idea; Ruth wasn't too sure. The little buildings had no windows or doors that could be closed, and she was concerned about the mosquitoes. I reminded her that we'd had dry weather for several weeks, so there were few mosquitoes. Reluctantly, she agreed to move us into the granary. We found a relatively clean place in a corner of the downstairs and spread out the sleeping bags that were dry. By this time the kids thought it was a great adventure. It was dark by the time we had them settled in for the night.

As Ruth headed back outside, I flashed my light around inside the granary and glimpsed something scurrying across the floor, along one wall. The light caught a field mouse's big ears and reddish brown back in its beam.

Nonchalantly I mentioned the mouse to Ruth.

"You saw *what?*" she said in a too-loud voice.

"Shh, you'll wake the kids," I cautioned.

"You saw a mouse in there?"

"Just a little field mouse, won't hurt anyone."

"I will not sleep in the same room with a mouse."

"It's only a field mouse," I said quietly.

"I don't care what kind of mouse it is. A mouse is a mouse."

I wanted to explain that field mice really are quite different from common gray mice, but this didn't seem the proper moment for an educational experience. We gathered up the children and drove the couple miles to my parents' farm to spend the night. We realized that we had more work to do before the cabin would meet Ruth's discerning criteria for what was and what was not livable. It was back to camping for us.

～～～～～～～～～～～～～～～～～～～～～～～～～～～～～～～～～～

Despite some challenges along the way, those years of camping at the farm were delightful— and educational as well, for Ruth and me and especially for the kids.

One clear July evening when we were camping in our usual spot, under a big black willow tree, I wrote in my journal:

Spiderwort in July

Temperature in the high eighties today. Tonight the whip-poor-wills are calling. One landed in the willow tree directly above the tent and thrilled the entire family. A few minutes later, I heard a deer snort, as they will do when they see something that doesn't look usual to them. An owl hooted in the woods to the north. A few horsetail clouds hung in the western sky; they turned to various shades of red, pink, and lavender and finally to black as the sun slipped away. Steam rose from the pond, creating an eerie cloud that hung over the valley to the west. Smoke from our campfire rose a few feet in the air, then trailed off to the south. Bats flitted about, catching mosquitoes. With total darkness, the sky was filled with stars and it was quiet, except for a few crickets that reminded us that fall was coming, and sooner than we wanted.

Those summer weeks camping at the farm helped me realize one of my reasons for wanting a piece of land—the opportunity for my children be in touch with nature, to experience a thunderstorm, collect wildflowers, swim in a pond, watch a turtle, listen to the crickets on a late summer night, and gaze at a sky filled with stars from one horizon to the other.

During one camping and cleaning weekend, the kids came running up to me to report on a little animal they had been feeding. "I think it's a chipmunk," Susie said.

I warned them to be careful about feeding wild animals, that sometimes they will bite.

"Not this one, Dad," Sue said. "He's tame."

While we were eating lunch under the canvas canopy we had erected over a picnic table, the "tame animal" appeared again for a handout. It was a thirteen-stripe ground squirrel, sometimes referred to as a gopher. The hungry little animal appeared to be living in the stone pile under the windbreak and just west of our campsite. The kids threw some bread crumbs on the ground, which the little creature quickly grabbed up.

The next day I saw the gopher slither out from underneath the tent. What was that little critter doing under our tent, I wondered. A few days later, when we took down the tent in preparation for our trip back to Madison, I saw that we had placed the tent over a gopher hole. No wonder the gopher was so close and so friendly; for a week we shared the same space.

We camped at the farm for several summers, until we had doors and windows in the granary, the mice and bats evacuated, and mosquito-proof screens. Now, living in the relative security of the refurbished granary that we had begun calling our cabin, the kids still asked occasionally, "When are we going to sleep in the tent again?" Even with the cabin somewhat livable, I would never forget the challenges we faced in making it so. Ole Knutson made it all possible.

A hand saw of the type Ole Knutson used to help transform the granary into a cabin

Chapter 14

<small>◇◇◇◇◇◇◇◇◇◇◇◇◇◇◇◇</small>

Cabin Building

"Dad, is this worth a whole-pail shower?"

THE APPS CHILDREN

"First thing to do is fix the roof," Ole Knutson had said when he inspected the granary. "No sense doing anything else when the roof leaks."

During my summer vacation in 1968, I pounded a new roof on the old granary. It was blistering hot, and even hotter on the granary roof. Each day I started roofing early in the morning and had to stop by noon when the temperature shot into the nineties. Total cost for the shingles: seventy-six dollars. I put them over wood shingles that were as old as the granary itself.

As I worked on the roof that summer, where it was hot but quiet, I couldn't stop thinking about the turmoil that was going on in Madison at the University of Wisconsin campus and around the country.

On April 4 Dr. Martin Luther King Jr. was murdered in Memphis. He was just thirty-nine years old. On April 5 rioting erupted in Chicago, Washington, D.C., Detroit—in nearly every major U.S. city. Yellow flames lit the city skies, and dark smoke billowed upward. Many states called out National Guard units to attempt to restore order. Federal troops ringed the White House; a machine gun was positioned on the White House lawn.

Ten thousand University of Wisconsin–Madison students assembled for memorial services on Bascom Hill, and fifteen thousand marched down State Street and around the Capitol Square. President Lyndon Johnson announced he would not run for a second term as Vietnam protests continued to escalate. It appeared the country had gone mad, had lost its bearings, as both civil rights marches and Vietnam protests escalated.

With all that going on, here I was pounding on a roof with only the sounds of songbirds and the breeze blowing through the black willow windbreak.

With the new roof in place, we could begin serious work on both the exterior and interior of the old building. We had salvaged several two-by-eights from the old barn that we planned to use for a new floor in the granary. We had also saved a four-by-four-inch oak beam. And we shoveled and swept out the accumulation of the years from the upstairs and the downstairs of the granary—old pieces of harness, broken glass, musty hay, dried manure, mouse and bat droppings, and baskets filled with unidentified items that best remained that way.

~~~~~~~~~~~~~~~~~~~~

With our busy schedules, nearly a year passed before we were able to return to our cabin work. When the university's spring 1969 semester ended, Ruth and I began scrubbing. We started upstairs, where mice and bats lived and where harness oil had soaked into the floor. Underneath the dirt and grime we found a beautiful pine floor of matched lumber. Its soft yellow-brown patina glowed in the sun shining through the broken window.

We scrubbed some more, with Pine Sol disinfectant in our scrub water, and slowly the musty upstairs took on the aroma of a pine forest, at least until the wood dried. We moved downstairs, scrubbing every square inch of every board, every two-by-four, every exposed surface with Pine Sol. So many people by now had told us that we'd never get the horse smell out of the old granary; we were out to prove them wrong. We scrubbed until we found clean wood, feeling like archaeologists digging through the years to find untold mysteries.

In July Ole Knutson came out to the farm to start us on our carpentry adventure. Ruth had given me a *Better Homes and Gardens* carpentry book for my birthday, and I had immediately begun studying its beautiful four-color photos and detailed instructions for how to do everything from putting a window in a building to constructing kitchen cabinets. I was feeling quite confident that I was no longer a mere know-nothing carpenter with zero experience. I had in my head the knowledge of the experts.

I showed my carpentry book to Ole. He scoffed, "Whatever those guys tell you, it won't work in this old granary."

"Why?" I asked meekly. I had depended on books for years to give me the knowledge I needed.

"Because those guys start with the assumption that everything is straight and true, and this old building is neither."

"Oh," was all I could muster.

"If you followed your book, the windows and doors wouldn't open or close."

"Oh," I muttered again.

"You gotta use a level for this building, just as much as you use a measuring stick," Ole said.

So began my carpentry apprenticeship. Ole had immediately seen that after years of withstanding the southwest wind, our granary leaned a bit to the northeast. Everything we did had to take into account that lean.

When Ole had agreed to our carpentry project, I had told him we had no electricity for his tools. "I'll dig out my old tools," Ole had said with a smile. "Good to be back using them, anyway."

On this day he proudly showed me a box of saws, all carefully stored and oiled so they wouldn't rust: a crosscut saw, a ripsaw, a finishing saw, and others whose names I've forgotten. Our first task was to install the big four-by-four beam across the ceiling of the first floor of the granary, to give it more stability. Ole measured the beam, marked the wood, and handed me a saw.

Anyone who knows anything about wood knows that sawing oak can be a challenge, especially dry oak. This old beam was more than fifty years dry. "Looks to me like you're a little soft," Ole said as my sawing slowed. "But you'll toughen up before this project is done." He was smiling.

When he arrived that morning, Ole had complained that his arthritis was bothering him. But he took the saw from me, and soon a pile of sweet-smelling sawdust had gathered at his feet. He hadn't even broken a sweat in the process.

We lifted the beam into place. It fit perfectly. "Lucky aces," Ole said.

Ole proclaimed, "Ladies and gentlemen, we now need a post to hold up this beam." We had a leftover piece of four-by-four, which Ole measured and I sawed—and sawed and sawed—until it was cut. All the while, I was thinking about what it would take to bring electricity into the place. The Coombes family never had electricity, so there was no wiring, no nothing, so we'd have to start from scratch . . .

We slid the post into place after lifting the beam a quarter inch or so with Dad's hydraulic jack.

"Make a good tight fit when we take the jack out," Ole said.

With the jack out, we nailed everything in place. "Time for a rest," Ole said. "No sense hurrying. Live a lot longer if you take your time. Do a better job, too. Hurrying makes for mistakes, and mistakes make for a poor building." This was just one of the many bits of wisdom the old carpenter had acquired over the years. During our years working together, Ole taught me many carpentry skills, but he taught me much more, as he was a storyteller and country philosopher.

Our rest over, we measured for the new door. By then it was noon. Ole joined Ruth, the kids, and me for lunch, which we ate under the canvas canopy near our tent.

Ruth made a sandwich for Ole, which he reluctantly accepted. "Never eat much lunch," Ole said. "Better to eat a big breakfast—eggs, bacon, a bowl of fruit, and toast. That's what I eat. Sets me up for the day."

Once he finished eating, Ole fished a can of tobacco out of one pocket and some cigarette paper out of another and hand-rolled a cigarette. The kids watched in amazement. Carefully, Ole shook some tobacco onto the thin paper, which he carefully held with one hand. Then he rolled the paper around the tobacco, wet one edge to seal it, and gave both ends a twist to hold the tobacco in. He found a kitchen match in one of his pockets, struck it on the side of his overalls, and lit the crude and crooked cigarette.

After lunch we worked on the door frame and cut the hole through the wall from the granary into the old chicken house. The three kids watched Ole's every move, and Susie, the oldest, peppered him with questions.

"What are you doing?" Susie asked.

"Making a door," Ole answered.

"Why?"

"So you can get into your cabin."

"Oh," Susie replied, as she and her brothers went off on another exploratory trip around the cabin.

Finishing with the door frame, Ole said, "About all we can do with the door until you get the floor in. I'll stop by tomorrow." He packed up his saws, climbed into his old car, and drove out the driveway.

The kids said they liked Ole and hoped they'd see him again. They liked the way he talked to them, asked them what they were doing, and didn't tell them to get out of the way when he was working. He took time to show them what he was doing. Ole liked children as much as he enjoyed carpentry.

I told the kids Ole would be back to work on the granary floor, which we had decided would consist of two-by-eights laid across the broken concrete floor and covered with particle board subflooring.

With the floor in place, Ole began installing a stairway to what would become the cabin loft. We spent the next morning cutting a hole in the upstairs floor for a new folding stairway.

"Looks good," Ole said when we had the hole cut and the stairs in place. "Now let's see if it works." Ole pulled on the rope to lower the stairway. The stairs stuck against the cabin wall halfway to the floor.

"Ladies and gentleman," Ole said. "Looks like we done something wrong." He unfolded his measuring rule.

"Forgot to take my own advice," he said, smiling. "Forgot to take into account the lean. Gotta move the stairway out from the wall a little, and it'll work."

That's what we did, and the stairway worked fine.

The next day Ruth and I began the work of insulating between the rafters upstairs, she holding and me stapling. It was a miserable job. When the steel wool insulation got next to sweaty skin, the itching became unbearable. But we labored on. I was thinking about how nice it would be sleeping here in the loft, away from the mosquitoes and the threat of water seeping into our leaky tent and soaking our sleeping bags.

At the west end of the building, I saw what looked like new mouse droppings on our freshly scrubbed wooden floor. Ruth quickly reminded me that neither she nor the children would sleep where mice lived. I assured her I would take care of the problem. Recalling the vast piles of bat dung we had swept from the granary loft during cleanup, I surmised that these were bat droppings, not mice leftovers. I kept quiet, and after Ruth had returned to the tent, I continued stuffing insulation in the west corner of the ceiling. My guess was confirmed. A fully grown brown bat with a furry body and black, skinlike wings flew out from its roosting place just before I covered it with insulation. I dodged as the bat swooped around the upstairs. Finally it found another roosting place.

The granary in the early stages
of restoration, 1968
PHOTO FROM THE AUTHOR'S COLLECTION

I continued stuffing insulation into the ceiling's many cracks and crevices. I found a hole to the outside and, guessing this was the bats' entrance and exit, I plugged it with insulation, confident I had solved the bat problem.

As the summer days passed, new windows appeared in the granary, both upstairs and downstairs. We put linoleum over the subfloor, covered the outside of the building with new siding, and scrubbed the former chicken house until all hints of chicken smell had disappeared— we hoped.

Ole Knutson came out nearly every morning, smiling wide as he showed me how to do the day's carpentry task. As the work progressed, I was able to swing a hammer most all day without tiring and saw a board without stopping. I was developing some confidence as a carpenter and feeling good about it—especially because we were doing the work the old-fashioned way, without using any power tools.

Ole stuck a sharp pin in my carpentry confidence balloon one day toward the end of summer as we were fitting in one of the last windows: "You know, Jerry, it's a good thing you're a teacher."

"Why's that?"

"Because you'll never make a carpenter. Look how crooked you sawed that board." He smiled when he said it, and I smiled, too; I knew he was right.

With the windows and door in place and new screens to keep out the flies and mosquitoes, the upstairs of the granary was ready for occupancy by the end of the summer of 1969. My mother gave us an old bed and mattress that we stuffed up the narrow stairway to the loft. We spread a canvas on the floor for the children's sleeping bags. As we looked forward to our first night sleeping in the cabin, Ruth and I felt very accomplished. After many nights in our old green tent, we were finally enjoying the result of our days of hard, sweaty work trying to remake this old granary into a cabin.

But that first night I had trouble going to sleep on a soft mattress. A soft breeze blew the length of the loft. I heard scratching. A tree limb rubbing on the roof? But no tree limb was near. A bird? Unlikely in the middle of the night. More scratching. I decided it was the bat trying to find its way in. So far, so good. Just scratching, no bat. I went to sleep and slept soundly, quite confident that no flying or crawling creature would invade the cabin loft. My confidence was premature. On a warm night a few weeks later, I awakened to the flutter of wings—another bat had found its way into the upstairs. With heavy leather gloves and a paper bag, I managed to catch it and take it outside. The next morning I searched again for small holes where a bat could enter. I plugged one tiny hole and hoped this would be the end of the bats. It wasn't, but our bat confrontations became considerably fewer as I continued to find and plug the occasional hole.

~~~~~~

Each year we continued to make the cabin more livable. With a neighbor's help we poured a concrete floor in the former chicken house lean-to, which was now our porch. In May 1970 we bought a used Home Comfort cookstove for fifty-nine dollars. The woman who sold it to us said she had paid three hundred fifty dollars for the stove only a few years earlier. The left side burned wood, and the right side had four gas burners—woodstove in the winter, gas stove in the summer. That summer I hired local electrician Cy Paine to wire the buildings for the day when we'd get electricity. It was much easier to string the wires in the cabin before we filled the spaces with insulation and nailed up the paneling. And with Ole Knutson's help, we finished insulating the downstairs of the cabin and put up wooden paneling on the walls and a tongue-and-groove board ceiling.

We repaired the pump so we would have a ready supply of drinking water, but we decided against indoor plumbing because of the cost of putting in a septic system and drilling a new well to handle the requirements of running water in the cabin. We were quite content to have a sturdy roof over our heads when the storms rolled in from the west, and a bug-free and reasonably bat-free place to sleep.

We kept the downstairs of the cabin as one big fourteen-by-twenty-foot room, with the cooking area on one end and the living area on the other. We organized the former chicken coop as a storage area; Leonard Erickson, another carpenter from Wild Rose, built us storage cupboards across the north wall of the porch. I used the south end of the porch as my writing area, and there I worked at a little desk in front of a window that looked out across the old farmstead to a little field where I often saw deer grazing.

We washed up with water from the well in a washbasin on a bench outside the pump house. We used plenty of Lava soap, the kind that tears at your skin, because we were constantly dirty from our various projects. The kids enjoyed drinking fresh well water, putting their faces in the cool stream as it poured out the pipe from the pump.

Showering was a problem without indoor plumbing. But we needed an efficient way to bathe, especially when we spent several days at the farm, gardening, cutting wood, and doing other arduous tasks, and I struck on the idea of building an outdoor shower. The kids and I hiked out to the black locust patch, where I cut three long locust poles, sixteen or eighteen feet each. We dragged them back to the cabin, and I set them up in tripod fashion, wiring them together so they would stand. I asked my neighbor in Madison, Maury Ellis, who owned a hardware store, to cut a hole in the bottom of a fourteen-quart galvanized pail, screw a sprinkler head on the end of a short garden house, and attach the other end of the hose to the hole in the pail.

We all used this water pail as a shower when we camped at the farm.

I fastened a small pulley to the top of the locust tripod, cut a shank of clothesline rope that I passed through the pulley, and tied one end to the handle of the water pail. We had a shower. Fill the pail with water heated on the woodstove. Pull the pail to the top of the tripod, stand under the showerhead, flip the little lever on the sprinkler head, and water poured down on you. We soon learned that three of us could shower one after the other using only one pail of water.

Of course, the whole contraption was right out in the open for all to observe our showering. The boys didn't seem to mind the arrangement, but Sue and Ruth said they wouldn't use the shower until I put up some kind of screen. I wrapped an old canvas around the tripod, and now everyone was happy, covered, and showering.

One of my incentives for the kids to help with garden work, especially hoeing, was the promise of a whole-pail shower. It became a standing family joke when I suggested chores to be done: "Dad, is this worth a whole-pail shower?"

Shortly after the wiring was completed, the local electric co-op put up a transformer and hooked us to the electric line. We had always stored our perishable foods in two ice chests filled with ice we purchased in Wild Rose, but now that we had electricity we purchased a used refrigerator. With the woodstove to heat the cabin on cold days, we were able to extend our season at the farm; we opened the place in April each year and closed for the winter after Thanksgiving. This we did for seventeen years, until September of 1987. By this time the children had grown, completed their educations, and left home. Ruth and I spent many summer vacation days at the cabin, gardening, bird-watching, hiking, mostly relaxing. The children joined us when they could.

In 1978 my brothers and I hired a surveyor and divided the farm into three equal sections of thirty-two acres each. Darrel, Don, and I would continue to jointly own 3.77 acres of land around the pond. At this time Donald lived in Sheboygan, and Darrel lived in Pennsylvania. Don camped occasionally at the farm; Darrel, because of the distance, seldom visited.

Starting in the early 1980s Ruth began hinting that we should consider indoor plumbing, even though the simple pump and the outhouse had served us well. The cabin wasn't large enough to accommodate a bathroom, and the wagon shed and corncrib that we used as a storage place was too small as well. And if we added a bathroom, we might as well add some additional living space.

Ole Knutson had died in 1981, at the age of eighty-two. Over the years my carpentry skills if anything had deteriorated. We needed another carpenter to help us. Someone suggested I call George Edgren, who lived east of Wild Rose and did carpentry, electrical, and plumbing work.

George suggested tearing down the wagon shed and corncrib and building an addition in that space. We designed a one-story addition, twenty by twenty feet, which would include a bathroom, a small living room, and a bedroom. The project required a new well and pump and a new septic system.

This time I felt no need to demonstrate my carpentry incompetence, and I stayed out of George's way, which I think he appreciated. By late summer of 1988, the addition was complete. We had indoor plumbing, a downstairs bedroom, and a kitchen with a sink. I was still writing at my little desk in the former chicken house, but I reminded myself that writers needed to suffer some.

With electric backup heat and two woodstoves, now we could keep the cabin open for the winter. We were at the farm one New Year's Eve shortly after George installed the living room stove. It was twenty below outside, and I had both woodstoves going full blast.

"Isn't it getting a little warm in here?" Ruth asked.

"Do you know it's twenty below outside?"

"Well, it feels like ninety degrees in here."

I checked the indoor thermometer: eighty-nine degrees. We began opening windows. What a sight it must have been for anyone driving by to see this cabin with smoke trickling from two stovepipes and all the windows wide open. I could hear the comments, "Must be a city guy living there."

In 1992 we asked George Edgren to add two more rooms to our cabin: a writing room for me and a craft room for Ruth. George completed this fourteen-by-twenty-foot addition in August 1993.

Around the same time, I purchased my brother Darrel's share of the farm, giving me about sixty-five acres. Now, with additional acres, I could do more with my prairie restoration as well as my various forestry projects. Darrel had a new business in New Jersey and welcomed the extra money from the sale of his portion of the farm. He kept his joint ownership of the pond.

Up to this time we had not had a phone at the cabin. It was time to put one in—not an easy task, as it turned out. I had appreciated all those years without phone interruptions, but now my aging parents required that we have a phone at the cabin.

The phone company representative came out, looked things over, and said, "Nothing to it," you'll have a phone in a few days. A day later, someone else from the company called me.

"We can't put in your phone."

"Why not?"

"Because you are in Wautoma territory."

"But my neighbor across the road is on the Wild Rose line."

"Your road is the dividing line. The west side of the road is Wautoma; the east side is Wild Rose."

"You mean I'll have to call long-distance to reach my neighbor?"

"I don't make the rules." He hung up.

I called the company that serviced Wautoma; their offices are in Sun Prairie. I told the woman what I wanted.

"Where did you say you live in Wautoma?"

"I don't live in Wautoma. My mailing address is Wild Rose."

"Then you should call the phone company for Wild Rose."

I patiently tried to explain that I had done that.

"We'll send someone out," she finally said. It turns out that we are about the last customer on the Wautoma phone system—the end of the line.

After several weeks the installers arrived on a day when I wasn't at the farm. They proceeded to bury the line not along the edge of our field but across the middle. When I saw what they had done, I once more called Sun Prairie.

"Let me connect you to our engineering department," the woman said.

After a few minutes of elevator music, a man came on the phone.

"How deep do you place phone lines?" I asked.

"Oh, several inches," he said. "Why do you ask?"

I explained that his installer had buried my new phone line across a field that I sometimes plowed.

"Well, don't plow there—you'll dig up the line."

"Could you move the line?" I asked patiently.

"We put 'em in; we don't dig 'em up."

My son Steve and I spent a half day digging up the phone line while another installer dug in the line along the edge of the field. At last, we had phone service.

Our cabin improvements continue. In 2005 we hired local contractor Bryen Edwards to re-side the cabin and put a new roof on both cabin and pump house. Bryen and his wife, Debbie, live in the old Floyd Jeffers house across the road. He is another skilled carpenter who pays close attention to detail. In pulling off the old cabin siding, Bryen discovered a huge colony of black ants on the north side of the old chicken house. These ants feed on old wood and were slowly destroying that part of the cabin.

Today the cabin is snug and tight, probably tighter than it's ever been. It's come a long way from the time it was a granary, chicken house, and horse barn. This old building has many stories to tell, so many more than I can tell, of the thirty-six years we have lived here. Stories of bats and mice, ants and hornets, and sleepy, rainy days when water dripped from the roof and the crackling woodstove fire stirred memories of when I was a kid on the farm. Stories I hope my children will never forget.

Stiff aster, a common prairie flower

Chapter 15

Roshara

"You've got to give the place a name."
ISABELLE DOWNIE, *WAUSHARA ARGUS* READER

In the spring of 1967 I began writing a freelance column for the *Waushara Argus*, a weekly newspaper for Waushara County and adjoining counties. In "Outdoor Notebook" I wrote about the environment and nature, country living, and rural history.

Our family's adventures at the farm became regular topics. I wrote about tree planting and brush clearing. I described the pond in summer and in winter. I wrote about skiing and sledding on our hilly acres, and about butterflies and squirrels and rabbits and wildflowers of many descriptions. I chronicled the children's encounters with bumblebees, garter snakes, and field mice. As readers became familiar with our farm and what we were doing here, they began asking for the name of the place. We variously referred to it as "the farm" or our "country place."

"You've got to give the place a name," Mrs. Isabelle Downie of Wautoma, who owned a small resort on Silver Lake, told me one day. "Town of Rose Farm is no name."

I tossed the idea back to the column readers. In an early October column I wrote, "I've got a problem and I think you can help. I need a name for our Town of Rose farm. And I will give a new bird guidebook to the person who suggests a name we like." I told readers we had thought of several names already; Ruth had suggested that we call the place Aching Acres in honor of our many days of hard work here. But we hadn't thought of the perfect name.

That fall I invited people to write a name for the farm on a postcard and send it to me at the *Waushara Argus*, deadline November 15. Once we received the cards, I said we'd hold a family meeting and pick out the one we liked best. The judges' decision would be final, I pointed out. I didn't say that to get five family members to agree on something as important as the name of a country place might take some doing. At the time I didn't think much about the decision-making process, either.

I expected that maybe a half-dozen people would send in cards and the whole process wouldn't amount to much. I also feared, a little, that we wouldn't like any of the names. But that's the chance you take when you ask other people for suggestions.

The postcards began arriving shortly after the October column appeared. I received cards from Lexington, Kentucky; Indianapolis, Indiana; Brookfield, Illinois; and of course from many places in Wisconsin. One correspondent sent in fourteen names on fourteen postcards. A woman from Neshkoro, a true skeptic, wrote, "Will you really choose a name sent in? I'll bet you'll use your own choice."

Several people wrote to tell me their stories. A woman from Plainfield, Wisconsin, wrote that her family had purchased seventy-five acres, with fields and woods and a house that was more than one hundred years old. "Most of the plaster was down," she wrote. "Mice, squirrels, and bees lived in the house—I thought I could never live there." They slowly turned the old house into livable quarters, much as we'd done with our granary. She ended her note, "We went to bed every night with a backache, and got up every morning with a backache, but it was worth every minute we put into it, to know we did it ourselves. We are very proud of the place."

We began sorting through postcards and letters, considering names like Nature's Nook, Rolling Meadows, Willow Farm, Laurel Hill, Pineview, Bit of Heaven, Green Briar, Nature's Haven, Apps' Rose Dale, Sleepy Hollow Farm, Wildwood Haven, Lupine Lodge, Rural Rose Retreat, and Shady Nook.

The cards kept pouring in over a period of several weeks. Just when we thought we had a name we liked, more cards would arrive and we would start over again. Idyll Wood Valley Farm, Dunbar, Buena Vista, Whispering Willows, Shady Willow Farm, Happy Hours, Yours and Ours, and Years and Hours (something about those last two names intrigued us).

A woman from Indianapolis who had grown up just down the road from our farm suggested Sha-Po-Pi-Ac. Has a nice ring to it when pronounced. The name is short for Shady-Poplar-Pine-Acres, and the first letter of each segment of the name spells Apps in reverse. Very clever.

I liked it. The kids didn't. Ruth was noncommittal. Vote: one for, three against, one abstention. "What else is in the pile?"

Mrs. Nedra Buelow from Wild Rose suggested Innisfree, from the 1920 William Butler Yeats poem "The Lake Isle of Innisfree." "I will arise and go now, and go to Innisfree, and a small cabin build there. . . . And I shall have some peace there, for peace comes dropping slow. . . . There midnight's all a glimmer, and noon a purple glow."

That was it. Innisfree had my vote. The Yeats poem captured so well my feeling about the farm. I read the entire poem to the family. They listened politely. The kids hadn't yet met William Butler Yeats in school. But they didn't think much of the name, and they had trouble pronouncing *Innisfree*. "What else you got, Dad?" Sue asked.

I picked up the postcard submitted by Ruth Pochman, who with her husband had a country place near Coloma. "I suggest Roshara," she wrote. "It's simple and it has meaning. It includes the first two letters of Rose, and the last five letters of Waushara."

Now heads were nodding. The kids liked the sound of it, and they could pronounce it. Ruth liked it, too. She said it had a kind of exotic, mysterious sound to it. But beyond the name's more superficial qualities, we liked its deeper significance. Roshara reminded us of the wild roses that grow along the fencerow above the pond. Wild roses have the sweetest of fragrances; no cultivated rose I've grown even comes close in aromatic qualities. Roshara also brought to mind those sturdy pioneers—including our own Tom Stewart—who moved from Rose, New York, and settled here prior to and just after the Civil War.

Looking north toward the pond

The Indian word *Waushara* is significant as well. It supposedly comes from the name of a local Winnebago Chief—Wau-shay-ray-kay-kaw—called Fox or Big Fox.[1] The name reminded us of the Indians who walked across these acres, camped at our pond, trapped, hunted, and fished here for hundreds of years before my family and I arrived.

We didn't even vote. It was a unanimous agreement. From that day on the farm would be known as Roshara—a rather extraordinary name for a very common, ordinary place.

PART III

Living on the Farm

Old road in fall

Chapter 16

◇◇◇◇◇◇◇◇◇◇◇◇◇◇◇◇◇◇◇◇

Old Road

"Two roads diverged in a wood, and I—
I took the one less traveled by,
and that has made all the difference."
Robert Frost

I've always been drawn to country roads—the kind that twist and turn and go up hills and down as they follow the lay of the land rather than plow straight ahead as modern-day roads are prone to do. Just such a country road trails by our farm. It is a mostly north-and-south road that follows survey lines, cutting section 33 in half until it drops down and makes a wide sweep around the east end of Chain O' Lake before climbing and heading north once more. It intersects with another country road, now County Highway A, that for years was known as the "old Indian Road" and was so noted by a government land surveyor in 1851.

Country roads were and are maintained according to their designation—town roads, county roads, state roads, and federal roads, each maintained by their respective governmental stewards. The higher the governmental designation, the greater the traffic, the straighter and wider the road, and the more boring the ride. On these more "modern" roads you can travel from here to there more quickly, which seems to be the goal of most people these days.

I learned by studying old plat maps that a town road once ran right through our farm, east to west. It intersected with the north-and-south road that runs by our farm. This abandoned town road once connected with another, now long-abandoned road to the west of our farm, providing easy access to the Ed Stickles farm. This mysterious road, no longer mapped, no longer maintained, and no longer traveled except by my family and me, follows the quarter-section survey line. I also discovered something called a Harrison monument alongside the road at the end of our farm. Early surveyors placed this Harrison monument, a metal pipe about two inches in diameter and sunk into the ground an unknown distance, to mark the corner of section 33, where our farm is located, and section 32, adjacent to the west.

A Harrison monument marks the corner of section 33, where the farm is located, and section 32 to the west.

I was curious to learn how the Harrison monument got its name. I thought it must be named after one of the Presidents Harrison— William Henry, ninth president, or his grandson Benjamin, twenty-third. I was betting on William Henry, known for obtaining title to Indian lands so settlers could move in. I searched many sources and read brief biographies of both presidents, but I couldn't find any connection between the Harrisons and the survey monument.

Finally I thought to ask Rob Nurre, land records manager with the State of Wisconsin Board of Commissioners of Public Lands, who squelched my romantic notions about a connection between the metal survey pipe on my farm and the president of the United States when he told me that Harrison is the family name of the company that makes them. Nurre did pass along some interesting details: "Rather than being a round tube with a survey cap at the top, Harrisons are cast as a stack of vertical and horizontal plats. The idea is that if the top of the monument is hit by a piece of farm equipment, the monument will break at one of the joints. Even if the top of the monument is broken off and displaced, the bottom of the monument will still be in place and the remaining portion still marks the survey corner." Although they are used in many locations, Harrisons were developed for use in agricultural areas, and surveyors use them to this day.[1]

The old road had once been graded, ditches had been dug, and some attempt had been made to cut down the hill that climbs west from the pond. Building the road must have been an onerous task, as all the work was done with horses and the simplest of earth-moving equipment. At one point these early road builders cut down a steep hill by twenty or more feet to make traveling the road possible. But even with the hill lowered, the climb is still steep.

I don't know when the road was built—my guess would be shortly after the Civil War—nor do I know when it closed. When I asked old-timers in the community if they remembered the road, most didn't, but those who did agreed that the road closed when automobiles replaced horses and buggies. I've also heard a tale about a rural mail carrier who delivered mail on this road for years using a horse and buggy, only to find the road impassable when he switched to a Model T Ford. These stories made sense. The road was sandy and very hilly, and early automobiles (present-day ones as well) would have had great difficulty negotiating the old road. Even with my tractor I stay very alert as I climb the hill beyond the pond and gaze into a ditch that falls off from the edge of road into a gully some twenty or more feet below the road.

The old road was eventually forgotten. It became Weston Coombes's field road, where his skinny cows walked on their way to a pasture that is now the prairie I am restoring. Remnants of old wire fence and cedar fence posts tell the story, enough of it at least so I can visualize the cattle trailing up the old road, one after the other, each morning and afternoon.

Bracket fungi grow on a dead tree.

Walking west on
the old road

The far west end of the road, the last few hundred yards, returned to trees, oak and poplar, some now more than a foot in diameter and thirty or more feet tall. I can easily spot the ditches and make out where the old road once went. Today, the first couple hundred yards of the road serve as our driveway. This segment has long since grown over to grass, as has most of the road. I keep the grass mowed in summer and the snow plowed in winter, so this part of the road gets constant use. We also regularly travel the road from our buildings to the pond. The upper part that climbs the hill to the former pasture gets used less often, mainly as a part of our trail system that winds around and through the farm and connects prairie areas with forested areas.

I am constantly challenged to keep the road passable as the dreaded buckthorn and black locust trees encroach on both sides for much of its distance. Near the pond, where the soil is heavier and less droughty, large-tooth aspen seek to grow in the road as well as alongside it. Wild grapevines grow in the canopy of tall aspen that line both sides of the road and meet overhead, providing hikers a cool, shady respite from the hot days of summer.

Besides providing a travel route to the back of our farm for my family and me, the road is a game trail where I regularly see deer, wild turkeys, ruffed grouse, the occasional woodcock, cottontail rabbits, and even a sandhill crane on occasion.

Today when I walk along this abandoned road, I imagine travelers from earlier years driving their horses and buggies on a Sunday afternoon to visit their neighbors. I can see Mr. Stickles, with his team and wagon, carefully negotiating the hill above the pond as he traveled to Wild Rose for supplies, perhaps stopping by to say howdy to Tom Stewart or waving to the Jeffers family on the other side of the north-south road. I can see the mailman, driving his enclosed buggy meticulously from farm to farm, delivering the mail no matter what the weather or the road conditions, six days a week.

Still useful today, this old country road holds untold stories of travel when horses and buggies were common and people were in no hurry to get where they were going. My grandchildren listen as I recount the likely uses of this old road, but they are more interested in today and the quick route it provides to the pond and its many mysteries.

Chapter 17

The Pond

"Guess what we saw, Mom?"

JOSH HORMAN, AGE TEN

A sandhill crane flies over the pond.

It has never been given a name but always referred to as "the pond." On some maps it appears, just barely; on others it is missing entirely. Yet it is a central feature of our farm, where something new is happening nearly every day of the year.

This small body of water, about five acres when the water table is high, is a mysterious, mythical part of our place. It is ever changing and always the same. It provides sanctuary for hundreds of birds—shelter in a storm for migrating ducks, geese, and even a pair of swans on one occasion. This is where all the wildlife in the area comes for water when rain is short and the land is parched.

For me it is also a spiritual place, especially on quiet mornings when wisps of fog lift from the still water and gather in little tongues that float on the surface. And in the evening, too, when the last robin sings and the water turns from blue to black as the sun slips behind the western hills. The stillness provides a time for uninterrupted reflection on my assorted problems and challenges and happy things as well. This is often the first place I go in the morning and the last place in the evening.

This dead tree is evidence of much higher pond levels.

As I stand by the pond on a rainy afternoon, each drop of rain creates a tiny whirlpool on the pond's surface and makes a tinkling sound like someone gently touching the upper-octave keys on a piano. By contrast, rain drips with a brusque thwack-thwack-thwack from the oaks and poplars and birches that line the shore.

Sitting quietly near the pond on a warm spring evening, I sometimes see deer coming down from the hills and woods for water, perhaps a doe with a pair of fawns still in their spotted coats but playful and unmindful of mama doe's direction. Or a mother raccoon and her brood, the little masked rascals carefully dipping their paws into the water, learning the ways of their parents.

If I am fortunate, and I often am, a mallard hen moves out of the rushes followed by a line of baby ducks, paddling furiously to keep up with mama but staying in a straight line behind her. All but one. There is always one that has another idea, another direction in mind. Mother duck turns around and swims back and chastises the naughty youngster, or so it appears.

The pond is a mysterious place all seasons of the year.

The pond's water level fluctuates with the years. In 2007 the pond was at the lowest level we've seen since 1967.

The pond is roughly ten thousand years old, just a youngster in geologic time, formed when a huge chunk of ice was buried by the last glacier to visit the area and then melted, leaving a depression that filled with water. It has neither an inlet nor an outlet but is fed by several springs on its south and west sides that bubble up year-round. Ours is a water table pond, which means its level goes up and down based on natural cycles of the water table—a great underground river of water known as an aquifer.

When we first acquired the farm, the pond was but a marshy area with little open water. Dad said, "I think we can improve this little lake." Although I was skeptical, I didn't say anything. My skepticism about improving on nature goes deep. Most of the time "improvement" results in further degradation.

What Dad had in mind was bringing in a dredge and deepening one end of the pond. With permission and some cost sharing from the government for wetland improvement, Dad hired a man with a dredge to dig out the mucky bottom of one end of the pond to a depth of eight or ten feet—and in so doing uncovered springs buried for years by several feet of soil that had washed into the pond from the nearby fields. The springs were an unintended bonus, and within a few years the pond was three times its previous size.

Over the forty years that we have owned the place, the pond level has gone up and down significantly at least three times. At its highest point, as recently as ten years ago, the pond had created an island with water flowing around the west side of a little knob of ground on which grew several oak and poplar trees. The high water killed birch and poplars all around the shore as each year the pond grew larger and larger. The little pond formed when Dad had the original dredged became a part of the larger pond. A survey post that had been on high ground was now several feet below the surface.

The pond is now at one of its low points in this mysterious water table cycle. The little pond to the southwest is nearly dry. The north end of the main pond has become marshlike again; new seedling trees once more grow where there had been water. The island is an island no more, merely a high point along the shore.

The pond is not only filled with bullheads, turtles, frogs, and assorted other water creatures, it is teeming with memories. Our three children spent many weekends and vacations swimming in its sometimes-murky waters, looking for creatures along its shores, canoeing every nook and cranny, fishing for bluegills, waiting quietly for deer to come for a drink on a warm summer evening, listening to the bullfrog chorus of loud "harrumphs" on an August night as darkness engulfed the valley that surrounds this little body of water.

The pond is also a place for surprises. One early spring morning, grandson Josh and I walked quietly to the east side, to the shore just down the hill from the cabin. I told Josh to walk as quietly as possible and not to talk, for the sounds of our approaching would spook any wildlife in the area. He nodded his understanding, and we shuffled quietly along the path, through the dewy grass of morning. The pond was as smooth and shiny as a tabletop. I caught a movement in the rushes on the far side, and I motioned for Josh to stop. A sandhill crane, a long-legged, four-foot-tall gray bird with a red cap, emerged from the tall grass and stood on the shore. We watched in awe. Josh had never seen a sandhill crane, probably had never seen any bird this large, especially this close.

Without warning, the crane began its mating dance. The huge bird flapped its wings and lifted its long legs high, trying to impress a mate we did not see. Watching this extraordinary event with my grandson was a highlight of the year for me. I couldn't wait to hear Josh exclaim to his mother, "Guess what we saw, Mom?"

Sandhill cranes hold a conversation at the pond.

Months later, on a cold, dark night in December, Josh, his brother Ben, their mother, and I walked through the dark to the pond, along the trail that threaded past naked oaks and poplars that were near invisible in the black night. I carried a flashlight but didn't turn it on, telling my grandsons that their eyes would adjust to the dark and they would be able to see their way in a few minutes. They did not believe me until minutes later they discovered that what had been black and invisible now had shape and form.

At the pond we walked on the smooth ice, the kids running, sliding, falling down, laughing, giggling, getting up, and falling down again. I shined the flashlight down through the ice and watched the beam filter to the bottom of the pond, where pond plants grew green and alive. Josh and Ben were amazed that light could penetrate ice.

We walked closer to shore, and I pointed out a muskrat run, where cunning muskrats had burrowed into the bank and formed an entryway into the pond. I saw the excitement on the boys' faces as I described how muskrats live in the pond year-round and what these little rodents eat and how well they can swim.

I was in the middle of my discussion of muskrats—interest was clearly waning on the part of my young audience—when it happened. A muskrat appeared under the ice and entered its tunnel. I turned the flashlight beam on this underwater swimmer. The reality of seeing overpowered my efforts at explanation. "Wow!" I heard. "Cool." Not often are my stories punctuated at just the right moment with the main actor coming on stage for an appearance!

We walked back to the middle of the pond, where the water was deepest. The boys' mother asked if the ice was safe out there, and I said that it was, for it was several inches thick. More sliding and falling down and giggling. The cold north wind was still that night, and a thin thread of a moon was visible in the black sky. Our sounds of merriment echoed in the valley as the pond waited for spring and young boys did what young boys have done for years—having fun without the need for equipment.

Without warning there was a loud noise, a sound like a rifle shot that pierced the quiet and echoed across the valley. At almost the same moment a crack formed in the ice, rushing past where the boys were playing. They heard the sound and saw the crack and knew for sure the ice was breaking. The boys yelled and ran for shore, their mother hurrying behind them. On shore I tried to explain that it was no more than a pressure crack, an expansion crack in the ice. "Think of the ice as talking to you," I said. My words meant little to boys now afraid of returning to their play. Soon, though, the boys had forgotten the loud cracking and were reluctant to return to the cabin—until they remembered that there waited hot chocolate and a grandmother eager to listen to their stories.

For me, sitting alone by the pond on a quiet evening or walking on the ice in winter, when the northwest wind sends slivers of snow hurrying across in ever-changing patterns, has meaning that transcends the words I use to describe the experience. The pond is one of the places on my farm where nature reaches into the depths of who I am, what I believe, and what I value. It is a quiet teacher, a patient listener, and a steady force.

This old apple tree is the sole survivor of an orchard likely planted by Tom Stewart in 1867 or 1868.

Chapter 18

✕✕✕✕✕✕✕✕✕✕✕✕✕✕✕✕✕✕✕

Apple Trees, Lilacs, and Daylilies

"In the dooryard fronting an old farm-house near the white-washed palings,
Stands the lilac-bush tall-growing with heart-shaped leaves of rich green,
With many a pointed blossom rising delicate, with the perfume strong I love,
With every leaf a miracle. . . ."

WALT WHITMAN

The tree looks like an old man, bald on top and with tufts of white on each side of his head. The analogy is about more than mere appearance, for this tree is extremely old as apple trees go, especially fruit-bearing trees. It grows alongside a little field to the south of the cabin, not far from where Tom Stewart built his original log house and barn and perhaps other log buildings I can only guess about. I want to estimate the age of the apple tree. I know Tom Stewart acquired this land in 1867; I know that he originally came from Wayne County, New York; I know it was common for New Yorkers and others who settled in what was known as Western country to bring apple trees and other plants with them. Apple growing was common in the East from colonial days, and like New York and New England, Wisconsin provided hospitable growing conditions for fruit trees, especially apples. Settlers like Tom Stewart commonly planted small orchards near their buildings. Thus, my guess is that this apple tree was planted in 1867 or thereabouts, making it more than 135 years old. The tree is likely the oldest living connection we have to our land's original homesteader.

When my family bought this land in 1966, four or five apple trees bordered this acre-sized field that at one time included barnyard, clothesline, vegetable garden, and perhaps some flower beds besides the log buildings—but I'm guessing again. What I know for sure is that this apple tree is so old that its main trunk is dead and broken off. Four or five years ago I found the top of the tree in a field, cracked off in a windstorm. It's the end of the tree, I thought. But it lived on, the remaining center trunk now mostly dead and scraggly where the broken trunk thrusts upward. There was enough life left in the old original trunk to send out side branches, and those branches continue to bloom and bear fruit.

Early settlers to Rose Township, many of them from upstate New York, brought with them daylilies, lilacs, and apple trees.

Tom Stewart may have also brought daylilies, orange and yellow ones, from New York, as daylilies grow in profusion around our old pump house and in another patch a few yards farther south. Tom's daughter, Ina, probably moved the daylilies when the family abandoned the log buildings and the old farmstead and constructed new buildings a few hundred yards to the north. But even as the old buildings fell into disrepair, the daylilies continued on undaunted.

Native to China, Japan, Korea, and eastern Siberia, daylilies were cultivated long before the birth of Christ. Some early Chinese records claim that daylilies were used to relieve physical as well as mental pain. The juice extracted from daylily roots supposedly quieted the heart, lungs, liver, kidneys, and stomach; benefited the mind; strengthened willpower; reduced worry and body weight; and brightened the eyes—all in addition to providing a splash of color to Chinese gardens. What more could one ask of this lowly plant?

The daylily's botanical name is *Hemerocallis*, from the Greek *hemera* (day) and *kallos* (beauty). Daylilies made their way to Europe along with spices imported from the Orient. By the 1500s daylilies were popular in Europe, and they crossed the Atlantic with the Pilgrims. The tawny orange daylily moved west with the settlers and became known to some as the homestead lily.[1]

Lilacs grow in front of the black willow windbreak, no doubt planted by the Coombes family after they constructed their new buildings. In late May they flower, deep purple, lighter purple, and white. The scent of lilac on a warm spring evening is one of the treats we look forward to each year, unless a late frost has killed the flowering buds, which happens one year in five. But even with a frost some of the lilacs will manage to bloom and let us know they are

Apple blossoms appear each spring on the old apple tree that once stood behind Tom Stewart's farm buildings.

there with their sweet aroma. We always have a big bouquet of lilacs on the cabin table when they are in season, their subtle spring smell mixing with aromas of wood smoke from our wood-burning kitchen range.

Lilacs originated in Turkey; their name comes from the Arabic *laylak* or the Persian *nylac*, meaning blue. The botanical name *Syringa* is from the Greek *syrinx*, a pipe. The shrub can grow to twenty feet and has pithy stems that can be hollowed out. The Turks apparently used the stems as pipes.

Lilacs are long-lived and require little or no care. Like apple trees and daylilies, lilac roots made their way west with settlers. "American settlers planted lilacs in front of farmhouse doors, not for usefulness but for beauty, while they struggled to make a new life in the wilderness. Sometimes the slowly cleared fields, the houses, and the walls were no more permanent than those who made them, but the lilacs remained by the ghost porches, leading nowhere."[2] Today it is easy to spot a former farmstead, even if all the buildings are gone. Look for a clump of lilacs. They are tough and persistent.

Our apple tree, daylilies, and lilacs are living connections to the history of our land, reminding us year after year of earlier days and the people who farmed these sandy acres before us—people who enjoyed the smell of lilacs on a warm spring evening, the splash of daylily orange in early summer, and the sweet taste of fresh apples in fall.

Chapter 19

Wildlife

"Who cooks for you? Who cooks for you-allllll?"

BARRED OWL

A wild turkey will lay ten to twelve eggs, but because the nest is on the ground,
predators will take many of them.

People who live in the country take wildlife for granted, as well they might, for the wild animals and birds are our neighbors and often are integral parts of our lives. But that doesn't mean wild creatures don't surprise us. Wildlife is as unpredictable as your most eccentric neighbor.

One early spring morning I was trudging along a trail on the far west side of the farm in a planting of red pines, half asleep and daydreaming. Suddenly I noticed something blocking the trail, a hulking brown creature about two feet long, with white stripes on its head—a badger. The hype about Wisconsin's mascot fails to point out that these low-slung creatures, with fierce claws, are not particularly friendly. My dad often told about confrontations between dogs and badgers; the badgers always won, no matter now mean or aggressive the dog.

I stopped. The badger stopped. We stared at each other for probably half a minute or so, although it seemed like half an hour. Then the badger walked toward me, choosing to challenge this tall, upright creature that it had seldom seen in this part of its territory.

I turned around and quickly walked in the direction I had come, glancing over my shoulder occasionally. I kept walking until I couldn't see the badger anymore. I don't know where or when it turned off the trail and forgot about me. Since that encounter I have found several badger dens on the farm, but that was the first and only time that I came face-to-face with a badger.

The wildlife at our farm enriches our lives. We enjoy the deer (mostly—see the gardening chapter), the wild turkeys, and even the coyotes howling at night. Raccoons—as cute as they are with their little black masks—and woodchucks (also called groundhogs) are pests and problems. The raccoons have an uncanny ability to know when my sweet corn is at its absolute peak for picking and eating. I believe they also know when I plan to pick it, for on several occasions I have trekked out to the garden with pail in hand to discover that raccoons visited the night before, stripping off the ears and sometimes even knocking down the stalks.

Woodchucks are also garden raiders, eating the tops of beets, devouring my lettuce, and attacking my green beans. Some of the garden eating is best blamed on our considerable number of cottontails, but the rabbits seem content to dine on new grass and generally leave our garden alone. Woodchucks are gifted hole diggers, and yes, they do enjoy living under woodpiles, especially mine. A couple years ago a full-grown woodchuck burst out from under our woodpile when Steve and I were moving the wood into the pump house in fall. The only other time I've been as startled was the year a four-foot garter snake slithered out from beneath the woodpile.

Upon entering my pole shed one spring day, I saw an immense pile of dirt under my canoe, which rested on the dirt floor. We moved everything out of that part of the shed and began digging to find out what critter had done the dastardly deed. We exposed an elaborate den; outside we found the corresponding hole that the woodchuck had used to travel under the shed wall and into the building.

Last fall I noticed a pile of dirt in front of the pump house, now our woodshed. A large tunnel went under the wall and footing to the inside. I found yet another pile of dirt alongside the wall for the well, which is some eight feet deep and surrounds the pipe for the pump. This critter, probably another woodchuck looking for a cozy place to spend the winter, gave up after digging some four feet and finding it couldn't get under the wall. I don't yet know if the woodchuck gave up entirely and left in search of an alternative home or will be back with a new plan. Time will tell.

Black bears are becoming a more common presence near our farm, as their numbers have dramatically increased in the state and they have ventured ever farther south in search of food. Autumn, when the bears are preparing for their winter hibernation and are foraging near and far, makes them bold, and garden produce and birdfeeders are easy picking. For the most part, black bears aren't a danger to humans, but they can be a nuisance as they search for food near human dwellings.

A few years ago a neighbor a half mile or so to the north found herself nose to nose with a big bear outside her kitchen window. Another neighbor who raises bees told me that bears essentially destroyed his bee yard a couple summers ago. One day in October 2005 my neighbor Bryen Edwards, who lives across the road, asked if I'd had bears at my birdfeeder, which then stood on a post outside my cabin window. I told him that I'd had to replace the feeder because it had been pretty much destroyed by some critters. I was blaming it on the wild turkeys that often visit my birdfeeder. But Bryen said, with certainty, "Bear—it was a bear that did it." He and his wife had recently watched a female bear and her cub as they snacked at his birdfeeder. Bryen and his wife weren't sure what to do, if anything, so they just watched, and soon the mama bear and junior wandered off across the field to the south.

Last September my brother Don, who lives less than a half mile from my cabin, stopped by to tell me a pumpkin story. A few days earlier he had arranged four big pumpkins and a few stalks of corn on his front porch as an autumn decoration. The next morning he noticed that one of the pumpkins was missing. He found the pumpkin smashed, with all of its seeds missing, near his machine shed, a couple hundred yards from his house. Then he discovered that one of his birdfeeders was nearly destroyed and another tipped sidewise. And in his garden he found squash smashed, with their seeds missing—and a big bear track in the soft soil. No question, a bear—a big bear—had paid him a visit in the night.

In mid-October the pumpkin-snatching bear returned and stole another pumpkin from my brother's porch while he and his wife slept but a few feet away on the other side of a house wall. Has this bear developed a special taste for pumpkin? It was likely the same bear, but we'll never know for sure.

~~~~~~

Our wildlife adventures continue through all seasons of the year. On a recent snowy mid-February morning, I strapped on my snowshoes and set out along the trail that leads from the cabin to the pond. A January thaw had melted much of the heavy December snows, leaving behind about four inches of crusty icy-snow mixture. Perfect for snowshoeing but near impossible for walking, as you'd fall through the crust with each step.

It had snowed about two inches of fluff the day before, and it was snowing lightly as I plodded along the trail toward the pond, working leg muscles I seldom use. The landscape was a study in quiet: cottony snowflakes, motionless trees, frozen pond. No birds calling, no animals moving with cracking of brush. Just the crunch, crunch sound of my aluminum-framed snowshoes.

I saw tracks where a deer had cut across the trail on its way to the deep woods to the north. Then I picked up the tracks of a coyote that had walked down the trail earlier this morning in search of breakfast. Coyotes are nearly twice the size of foxes, weighing up to thirty pounds and as long as fifty inches, including a bushy tail that may be sixteen inches long. You'll seldom see their grayish form, though, because they are both largely nocturnal and extremely shy. This coyote track was larger than a fox's and smaller than a gray wolf's, which we have not yet seen at the farm. (The nearest wolf pack, according to the Wisconsin Department of Natural Resources, is about twenty miles west of our place.)

In the past five years we've seen coyote numbers increase dramatically. We hear them regularly at night, yapping with a high-pitched bark and occasional howl. Their call unnerves those who come to the country from the city and don't know its source. Some of our urban friends become even more anxious when they learn that what they are hearing is a coyote. Coyotes don't attack people. But if the visitors happened to bring along their pet miniature poodle, they would be well advised to bring Muffy inside; a coyote feeds on small animals and doesn't know Muffy from Peter Cottontail.

The coyote tracks turned off the main trail and led up a steep path that cuts alongside the black locust patch before it levels off at the top of the hill and leads south, joining the prairie trail. At the top of the hill, in a small clearing, coyote tracks were everywhere—then I found the reason. One spot of blood on the white snow. The coyote had found its breakfast. I looked for the victim's tracks, but I couldn't figure out what animal had been killed. Nevertheless, it was clear evidence of nature's way, animals eating other animals in order to live through the long winter.

I trekked on, through the red pine plantation that we had recently thinned and on along the white pine windbreak before turning down the hill toward the cabin. It felt good to be on snowshoes, reliving the days of those travelers who needed them to walk across the snow-covered expanses of the north. Back at the cabin, I unbuckled my snowshoes, shifted my boots out of the bindings, and pulled off my parka and cap. I stuffed another stick of split oak wood in the cookstove, poured a cup of coffee, and watched the snowflakes flutter earthward.

~~~~~~

One July evening a couple summers ago, I sat on a bench at the west side of the prairie, on the trail I'd mowed with the tractor a week earlier. It had been a hot, steamy day with temps in the low nineties. The sun had been down a half hour or so when I saw the little doe approaching, probably last summer's fawn.

She came from the south, walking quietly through the tall prairie grass and stopping occasionally to eat. Moving slowly, she got to the trail about a hundred yards in front of me, stopped, and looked in my direction. She didn't move. Nor did I.

For a minute or so we stared at each other. Then she jerked her head up and down several times. I remained motionless. She walked toward me, four deliberate steps, and stopped again. And we stared at each other. Again she moved her head up and down, trying to catch my scent, watching me closely for a reaction. She repeated this ritual four times, until she was a scant fifty yards from me. I remained as motionless as I could. There was not a hint of a breeze this evening, so the young doe could not smell me. She seemed both baffled and curious about this figure she saw but could not hear or smell.

She flicked her ears back and forth, her head high as she tried to catch my scent. Now she turned away and walked back into the tall prairie grass, still keeping an eye on me. She circled, coming closer and closer. Now she was only thirty-five or so yards away, the prairie grass nearly to the top of her back. We both stared.

A whitetail deer feeds in the field next to the pond.

Then came a hint of a breeze, and almost immediately the doe caught my scent. She leaped straight up in the air and at the same time turned half around. Her white tail came up, and she bounded toward the east in giant, beautiful leaps on legs that had become springs.

With a few graceful bounds she arrived at the edge of a wooded area, now some two hundred yards from me. Once more she turned toward me; I still had not moved. She lowered her tail and snorted loudly, the sound echoing through the steamy valley. She snorted once, twice more. And then she looked for a reaction from me.

In a minute or two she slipped into the woods and disappeared. I remained motionless, and in a scant few minutes she emerged from the woods and went back to eating prairie grass. She had either forgotten I was there or decided to ignore this motionless guy on top of the hill who insisted on watching a lady eat her supper.

Over the years I've seen many deer at Roshara, but seldom this close to me. I learned long ago that early evening is a good time for deer watching.

~~~~~~

Neither Ruth nor I are serious bird-watchers; we don't travel to exotic places with bird-watching in mind or keep lists of birds we've identified. Yet we love the birds at our farm in all seasons of the year.

Our bird season starts with March's lengthening days. The cardinals call at daybreak, their clear whistle starting my day on a high. By mid-March I hear the first ruffed grouse in the woods to the north of the farm. Its wings pound slowly at first, then more rapidly, like an old John Deere tractor. Later in the month, the first Canada geese are winging over. The "gobble, gobble" of wild turkeys—they have been quiet all winter—tells me spring is near. About the same time I hear the sandhill cranes calling, and I know they are back from their winter quarters. The sandhill crane's rattling call is one of a kind; some say the bird sounds like it has a sore throat. For me the sandhill's cry is delightful, haunting and prehistoric—a reminder of dinosaur days when giant creatures walked the earth and enormous flying creatures blotted out the sun. A pair of sandhills nests on the west side of our pond every year.

In spring we see red-winged blackbirds and killdeer at the pond, great blue herons wading along the shore looking for minnows, and the smaller green heron, with its piercing call. Mallards and wood ducks return to the pond by April. We have constructed houses for both species, on posts in the water so that predators have difficulty getting to them.

Usually on a cold, blustery day in late March we see our first robin, its feathers all fluffed up as it searches for insects on the bare, brown grass in front of the cabin. By April the migrant birds are passing through, flocks of warblers that rest in our willow trees for a few days before moving on north.

The bluebirds return in late March or early April. We put up our first bluebird houses forty years ago. Now each year we replace those that have clearly seen better times with new ones, bolted to black locust posts that we cut from the locus patch. Every year about 20 percent of our bluebird houses will have bluebirds. The rest are claimed by tree swallows.

With the arrival of May and warmer temperatures, our summer

A tree swallow pokes its head out of one of many bluebird houses at Roshara. Tree swallows often nest in unused bluebird houses.

birds begin returning to the birdfeeder hanging in the white spruce just outside the cabin window. Along with the cardinals and nuthatches that overwintered, we now see rose-breasted grosbeaks, indigo buntings, mourning doves, and goldfinches.

WILDLIFE AT ROSHARA

- **badger** (*Taxidea taxus*)
- **beaver** (*Castor canadensis*)
- **black bear** (*Ursus americanus*)
- **brown bat** (*Eptesicus fuscus*)
- **coyote** (*Canis latrans*)
- **deer mouse** (*Peromyscus maniculatus*)
- **eastern chipmunk** (*Tamias striatus*)
- **eastern cottontail rabbit** (*Sylvilagus floridanus*)
- **eastern gray squirrel** (*Sciurus carolinensis*)
- **flying squirrel** (*Glaucomys sabrinus*)
- **fox squirrel** (*Sciurus niger*)
- **house mouse** (*Mus musculus*)
- **mink** (*Mustela vison*)
- **muskrat** (*Ondatra zibethica*)
- **raccoon** (*Procyon lotor*)
- **red fox** (*Vulpes vulpes*)
- **red squirrel** (*Tamiasciurus hudsonicus*)
- **river otter** (*Lutra canadensis*)
- **striped skunk** (*Mephitis mephitis*)
- **thirteen-lined ground squirrel** (striped gopher) (*Spermophilus tridecemlineatus*)
- **white-tailed deer** (*Odocoileus virginianus*)
- **woodchuck** (*Marmota monax*)

One year the Apps children found a cottontail rabbit's nest near the lilac bushes. Predators had taken all but one baby rabbit.

PHOTO FROM THE AUTHOR'S COLLECTION

Many other summer birds do not come to the feeder. Baltimore orioles build elaborate hanging nests in our willow trees, and house wrens take up residence in the little birdhouse outside the kitchen window. Their happy chatter often wakes us in the morning. Gray catbirds nest in the willows. They meow like a cat and also mimic the calls of other birds, sometimes letting loose with a delightful repertoire of mixed birdsong. Occasionally we spot a ruby-throated hummingbird flitting around the rosebush by the corner of the cabin, its filmy wings moving so rapidly we can scarcely see them.

On a hot day in summer I'll often spot a red-tailed hawk sailing over my prairie, its wings motionless as it rides the updraft thermals. I'm reminded to look for it when I hear its piercing "kee-wee" call. And on a hot, still summer night, the whip-poor-will calls its own name over and over again, sometimes ten or more times in a row. We seldom see this reclusive, ground-loving bird, but its call is unmistakable as it echoes through the valley west of the cabin and lulls us to sleep.

With the coming of fall, our summer birds begin disappearing, winging their way to warmer climes. Great skeins of Canada geese fly high overhead, their call reassuring—for some things are still right with the world as long as the geese make their seasonal migrations.

On frosty October evenings, when the sky is so clear that you could count every star, a barred owl calls from the deep woods to the north: "Who cooks for you? Who cooks for you-allllll?" Often the call is answered from a different direction. Are these love calls in the night, I wonder.

With the passing days of autumn and the first snowfall, our winter regulars begin returning to the birdfeeder, assured of something to eat when their supply of weed and wildflower seeds become buried in snowdrifts. Chickadees, friendly little birds with a black cap and a winter personality, will face whatever weather is thrown their way and joyfully sing their name over and over. They usually appear first, flying in from the protection of the lilacs near the black willow windbreak. They sit on a lower branch of the big spruce, waiting while I fill the feeder. No matter how cold or how snowy, they always greet me with a cheery "chick-a-dee-dee-dee." Juncos, sometimes called snowbirds, appear next. With slate gray backs and whitish bellies, they gather on the ground under the feeder to eat what others have spilled. Soon we see white-breasted nuthatches, an occasional downy woodpecker, brilliant red male cardinals and the more muted females, and bluejays, often the bullies at the feeder, forcing others away while they devour what they want.

Wild turkeys have become common at the farm.

Usually at dusk, when a gray winter afternoon slowly becomes darker as the unseen sun begins to set, several wild turkeys sneak in quietly from the field to the west to feast on the feeder leavings on the ground. Later, deer will do the same thing. Turkey and deer tracks in the snow give them away when I walk by the feeder in the morning on my way to the woodshed for an armful of stove wood.

The work of a pileated woodpecker on a dead pine tree

No matter how cold or miserable a winter day, crows are always present, calling from the tops of a tall cottonwood trees near the pond, flying over the snow-covered prairie, roosting in the white pine plantation. A bird seldom praised, the crows' presence is one constant when other wild creatures are hunkered down, waiting for warmer temperatures.

Sometimes on a quiet winter morning, I hear the loud "rat-tat-tat" of a woodpecker looking for breakfast, a grub or worm in a dead tree. Several times in recent years I've watched a pileated woodpecker work. The pileated is our largest woodpecker, sixteen to nineteen inches tall with a wingspan up to thirty inches and boasting black with white neck stripes and a prominent red crest. It is a beautiful creature—and an effective wood chiseler. It not only pounds holes in dead trees (it seems to prefer pines and poplars), it chisels out rectangular holes in live trees as well, sometimes three or more inches long and an inch wide. It's easy to spot a pileated woodpecker's work; just look for a pile of wood chips gathered at the base of a tree, scattered on the white snow. But catching the bird at work is a challenge, as it is shy and prefers working out of sight. By following the sound of the pounding and creeping along quietly with binoculars in hand, I've been able to watch this woodpecker work for fifteen minutes or more before it senses me and flies off, letting go with a loud "cuk-cuk-cuk" that echoes through the woods on a cold morning.

The wild animals and birds have been our constant neighbors here. Except for a few neighborly misunderstandings, especially concerning my garden, we have gotten along well. How drab the countryside would be without them.

Chapter 20

Characters

"Glad you bought this place. Good to have a neighbor again."

FLOYD JEFFERS

Bill Boose of Wild Rose painted a picture of the farmstead in 1971.

It's more than a truism that neighbors are an important part of rural communities. They always have been; they continue to be so. I grew up in the same neighborhood where my farm is located, so I have known people here for many years. I went to country school and high school with some of them. I worked on threshing crews with them, helped them saw wood in the early days when we all heated our farm homes with woodstoves, and celebrated with them on the Fourth of July. Some of them were real characters.

Floyd Jeffers lived across the road from the farm I now own when we bought the place. Even though he died in 1970, we all have fond memories of Floyd, as he liked to be called.

Floyd Jeffers's farm was but a couple miles from my dad's farm, and I had known Floyd since I was a boy. In all that time he had lived alone in a house built by ancestors who came to Rose Township from Rose, New York, in the mid-1800s. Floyd's farm was not prosperous. In addition to the old farmhouse, Floyd had a small barn built into a steep side hill so that his cattle could enter the bottom of the building and Floyd could easily haul hay into the haymow on top of the hill. The farmstead included a couple of other small buildings, plus a shed built over his pump. Floyd wasn't much for improvements. He farmed mostly as his ancestors had farmed, with a team of horses and horse-drawn tilling and harvesting equipment. His income, meager as it must have been, came from a small herd of Guernsey cows that he milked by hand twice a day.

Floyd mostly kept to himself, but not because he wasn't neighborly. It just was difficult for a bachelor to fit into neighborhood social situations, which usually involved husbands and wives and their children. Floyd belonged to the Wild Rose Historical Society, which met monthly (still does). Other than that, he was home most of the time.

Floyd Jeffers was thin and bent over for as long as I knew him. He walked with a walking stick he'd cut from an oak branch. When he stopped to talk, he planted the walking stick in front of him and put both of his big, gnarled hands on top to support himself. Floyd had a long, thin face with a prominent jaw and deep, penetrating gray eyes. Some said his eyes looked right through you. He didn't smile much, mostly because he didn't have much to smile about, I would guess.

Some neighbors thought Floyd was strange and made disparaging comments about him—living all alone and across the road from the equally strange Coombes family, a mother and son living under the most primitive of conditions. My dad, though, talked to everyone in the community, whether they were thought strange or not. He believed that you had to know your neighbors. "Never know when you might need a neighbor's help," Dad said often.

Most of the people who spoke negatively about Floyd Jeffers didn't know him and probably had never talked to him. If they had, they would have discovered that Floyd was one of the most well-read people in the community. He read magazines, books, and several newspapers. And he could talk about news events, history, nature, whatever you wanted to pursue—except most people didn't talk with him at all. Floyd talked rather slowly and deliberately, and when he said something it was usually more than a comment about the weather. He liked to talk about what he was reading. Most of his neighbors didn't talk about what they read, not much anyway.

Visiting Floyd's place occasionally with my dad, I saw firsthand his piles of newspapers, magazines, and books everywhere—on the tables and chairs, on the floor, in the corners. Everywhere. We had to make our way through the maze of narrow alleys between stacks of reading material.

At a time when nearly all of our neighbors, including my family, hunted and roamed widely over each other's farms in search of game, Floyd Jeffers had posted No Trespassing signs around his sandy land. He didn't hunt, and he didn't want others to hunt on his property. Many of Floyd's neighbors resented his signs. But Dad respected his decision. "If he doesn't want us to hunt on his land, that's his business," he said.

Floyd developed a reputation for caring more for wild creatures than for himself. Some neighbors said that when he came home after shopping for groceries he had a small sack of food for himself and several sacks of feed for wild birds and animals. He kept several birdfeeders and feeders for other creatures—unheard of among our neighbors in the 1940s and 1950s. Wild creatures loved the man. Chickadees ate sunflower seeds from his fingers. Squirrels ate corn at his feet.

In 1966, when we bought the Coombes place from my dad, Floyd Jeffers still farmed across the road. He was in his midseventies by then and bent over even more than I had remembered him. One hot day in August 1967, when I was doing some work around the old granary building and the rest of the family was off swimming at Silver Lake east of Wild Rose, Floyd came shuffling across the road. "Glad you bought this place," he said. "Good to have a neighbor again."

We talked about earlier times when I was growing up on the home farm. And we talked about my dad and how they had known each other since they were both young fellows in the neighborhood. Eventually we got around to the Coombes place and discussed the problems we'd had taking down the old barn and our plans for converting the granary into living quarters.

"Sometimes hard to get the horse smell out of a building," Floyd offered.

"Others have told me that," I said. "But we're going ahead anyway." Floyd didn't say anything. He didn't need to. The look on his craggy face said it all. At the time I figured he thought we were a little strange to go ahead with the cabin project.

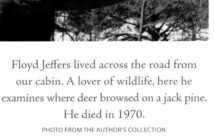

Floyd Jeffers lived across the road from our cabin. A lover of wildlife, here he examines where deer browsed on a jack pine. He died in 1970.

PHOTO FROM THE AUTHOR'S COLLECTION

In the shade of the big black willows, we talked for an hour or more, into late afternoon. Then Floyd said he had to go and shuffled off down my driveway, slowly and deliberately, leaning on his crooked oak cane.

Over the next few years, Floyd came over regularly when he saw me working in the yard. One time he came carrying a pail filled with several kinds of wildflowers he'd picked on his farm. "Found these near my woods," he said. "Don't know what they are." For the next hour we paged through my wildflower identification books, keying out Floyd's wildflowers.

He occasionally wrote me a letter, especially during the winter months when we spent more time in Madison, to let me know how things were at our farm. In January of 1970 I received a short note from Floyd, "All is quiet at Roshara, only thing I've seen lately is a doe deer walking across your dooryard." He told me that he was going into the hospital for some routine "repair work."

Floyd died in the hospital. In my newspaper column that week I wrote, "I lost a friend last week, an old friend and a good friend. Floyd Jeffers was 79 years old. He was active and interested in life until the very end. He was a link with the past . . . a real 'old-timer.' I'll miss him. I'll especially miss his visits to Roshara when we are there."

~~~~~~

Like Floyd Jeffers, folks around Rose Township considered Bill Boose unusual. The two men had some things in common; both loved the out-of-doors, and both were well read, aware of what was going on at home and in the larger world.

There the similarities ended. Floyd Jeffers spent his entire life on the same farm. Bill Boose moved around. Born in Jackson County, Wisconsin, he had lived in Waupun, San

Francisco, Seattle, British Columbia, and Saskatchewan. He'd worked as a farmer, as a bookkeeper, and as an attendant in the Waupun asylum for the criminally insane. And Bill was an artist—and a good one. Working in both watercolor and oil, he painted wildlife and wildflowers and still lifes of everything from pussy willows to dahlias. Bill had a considerable reputation among the rural artists of his day and was featured in the 1948 book *Rural Artists of Wisconsin*.

I met Bill through my dad, and not until Bill was in his late seventies, living on a small farm that he owned east of Wild Rose. He had mostly retired from farming but continued painting, trapping, and growing ginseng. Much of Wisconsin's crop of this exotic root is grown in Marathon County, but Bill grew it here and was proud to show me his ginseng patch whenever I stopped by.

Medium height and thin, with sharply chiseled features, Bill loved to talk about hunting, trapping, and his painting. He always wanted to know more about what I was doing at our farm and told me he read my weekly newspaper columns to keep up with our farming adventures.

Early in our years at the farm, I asked Bill if he would consider painting a picture of our farmstead, which at the time consisted of the granary and our old, well-aged pump house with the burned siding still on the south side. "Sure, love to do it," he said.

I was afraid I couldn't afford what he might charge me for the work—and I didn't ask. I did offer some photographs he could use as a guide for his work.

"I don't work from photographs," he said. "I want to see the real thing."

In the fall of 1971 Bill Boose began painting a picture of our farmstead. He set up his easel on a little hill south of our farm buildings, and he painted, day after day for most of a week, creating a large painting in oil. I began to really worry about the price—I even told him not to bother framing the painting when he'd finished it, that I would have that done myself. But he said, "I'll take care of the framing. Unless it's framed right, you'll spoil it." He didn't let me have one peek at the painting while he worked on it; he didn't want me to see it until it was finished and framed. Some of the neighbors asked me what that guy was doing, sitting on the hill south of my buildings.

"He's painting a picture," I said.

"Who is it?"

"Bill Boose," I answered.

"Oh," was the response, often with one brow raised. The implication was that I shouldn't expect much from Bill Boose. Of course, those who made such comments knew almost nothing about Bill's work. Many saw him as a rather lazy farmer who spent his time trapping and growing ginseng. Most folks had an opinion about Bill, and most thought he was unusual.

A week or two later, Bill called and told me I should stop by his place. He had finished the painting. "Turned out pretty good, too," he said. He was a modest man, not one to boast. But I could tell he was proud of what he had done.

Now I had to face the inevitable. What would he charge me? If it turned out to be several hundred dollars, I didn't know what I would do.

At Bill's studio, the painting stood on an easel. It was in a beautiful wooden frame.

"There she is," he said. "What do you think?"

"I think you've done one fine job," I said. And he had. He had captured everything from the barbs on the wire fence to the puffy clouds above the old granary. More than that, he had captured on canvas some of the emotion that I felt toward the farm and its buildings. I stood speechless for a moment as I gazed at the painting.

The moment of truth had arrived: "How much do I owe you?"

Bill hesitated. I imagined he was calculating the several hours he had spent at my farm.

"Would fifty dollars be okay?"

"More than fair," I said. "More than fair."

That Bill Boose painting, done in 1971, has hung above our fireplace in Madison for more than thirty-five years. When I look at it I'm reminded of the interesting man who did many things in his life, but always painted. Bill Boose died in 1978, seven years after doing my painting. He was ninety-one.

Chapter 21

◇◇◇◇◇◇◇◇◇◇◇◇◇◇◇◇◇◇◇◇◇

Gardening

"It's got to be right, Grandpa."

BEN HORMAN, AGE SEVEN

Onions in the garden

We planted our first garden at Roshara in spring 1967, and we've planted a garden every year since. For many years, especially when the children were still home, we planted up to two acres of garden each year. In the early years, gardening was a major endeavor that included selling produce at the Madison farmers' market and attempting to sell fresh vegetables to people vacationing at nearby lake cottages.

We situated our first garden, probably the largest of all, in the field west of the cabin. We harvested sweet corn by the bushel, potatoes by the wheelbarrow load, carrots by the pail full, and enough tomatoes to feed our city neighborhood and more.

My parents were excellent gardeners. My mother saw gardening as a way to put food on the table. Dad agreed with that, but he always viewed gardening as fun, too. Every year he planted something exotic—a vegetable of a strange color, some plant that no one had seen before in central Wisconsin, something that he could talk about with his neighbors.

I've tried to follow his example, planting something new every year. One year we tried Mexican corn. According to the seed catalog, the corn was supposed to grow ten feet tall; it grew much taller than that, so high—not an exaggeration—I had to stand on a stepladder to reach the ears. Another year when it rained regularly (most years our garden lacked rainfall and suffered because of it), we planted giant pumpkins and squash. In other years dry weather or bugs had killed them or I had "geed" when I should have "hawed" with the rototiller and torn them out. But this year the rains came often, and we grew eighty-pound pumpkins and squash that tipped the scale at more than 120 pounds. They were huge and grotesque, nothing to look at it—but they were big. For those who like *big*, these were it.

Ruth suggested we should try zucchini squash one year, in the days when summer squash and especially zucchini were not yet popular. I had never grown them. Neither had my folks—for them squash was something you harvested in the fall, stored in the cellar, and enjoyed throughout the winter.

In what quickly became known in our family as the "year of the zucchini," we put in a long row of zucchini, thirty or forty feet. I planted them as I would winter squash, giving them lots of room to grow and spread out. The rains came on time, the sun was warm, the pests were few, and the zucchini began growing and never stopped. The plants were soon three feet tall, dark green, and rather handsome. Soon the big yellow blossoms began appearing, followed by the fruit.

We still hadn't figured out what to do with zucchini. I assumed it was like winter squash, so we let it grow. And it grew and grew and grew some more. What looked like cucumbers on

Monday looked like green baseball bats on Friday. By the next Friday these long, green, and fattening fruits were four feet long and still growing. I decided to harvest some of them, cording them up in my arms as I would stove wood.

"Quite impressive," Ruth said. "But what do I do with them?"

"Bake them," I said. "They're squash, aren't they?"

I halved a giant zucchini, but I couldn't figure out how to remove the seeds as you would with a winter squash. I declared the entire project a disaster, an experiment that had clearly grown out of hand. I stacked the zucchini at the end of the garden row, and an impressive stack it was. I decided I would plow them under in the fall, give them back to the soil from whence they came as a fertility gift.

Shyly and discreetly I inquired of some gardening friends about what to do with zucchini. I didn't share that I now had a pile of zucchini three feet high and four feet wide, not unlike a stack of cut pulp wood ready for hauling to a paper mill. (I wish that paper mills had wanted zucchini; we would have prospered that summer.)

"Oh, zucchini is wonderful," one friend gushed. She proceeded to talk about frying zucchini (who ever heard of frying squash?), making zucchini bread and cake, and slicing them up in salads. "The little ones are best, those six inches or so long," she said. I didn't share that our zucchini were as large as baseball bats and bigger.

One year the rains came regularly and the squash grew large.
Left to right: Jeff, Sue, and Steve in 1972.
PHOTO FROM THE AUTHOR'S COLLECTION

"You only need two or three hills, and you'll have all you want," she added.

How about twenty-five hills, I wanted to reply, but didn't.

Sunflowers provide a splash of fall color in the garden.

We have planted and enjoyed zucchini every summer since. I plant four or five hills and pick the zucchini when they are only a few inches long. Ruth bakes zucchini bread—a favorite of our grandchildren, who prefer zucchini bread over apple pie. We eat it raw in salads (I must confess it's an acquired taste, or better said, no taste at all). We have fried it—not too bad if you add lots of onions. It's good grilled, too. Like everyone else who grows zucchini, we give lots of it away. Try to give it away, that is.

One late summer we decided to peddle some of our produce house to house. We loaded the car with new potatoes, fresh-picked green beans, and several proper-sized zucchini and headed to the lake country east of Wild Rose. The kids would do the selling—after all, who could turn down three little tanned, towheaded kids with produce to sell?

I remembered the days when my brothers and I tried to peddle rutabagas house to house and sold almost none. It was a wonderful lesson for us, trying to sell something to people that they didn't want. But who could refuse fresh vegetables like green beans and potatoes?

Turned out I was right. Within an hour or two, the kids had sold everything we had in the car. A few people had turned them down, but not many. Their income came to about twenty dollars. We stopped at the drive-in restaurant in Wild Rose on the way back to the farm, and they spent their entire day's income. "Selling sure makes you hungry," eight-year-old Sue said.

Selling at the big farmers' market on the square in Madison, in the shadow of the state capitol, was even more interesting, and more lucrative. Farmers' market money became spending money for the children, divided evenly among them. On Saturday mornings, when they had other "more important" things to do, the money incentive kept them content at least for a couple hours. Every Saturday in fall, the kids and I sold pumpkins, squash, popcorn on the cob, and even walking sticks I had made from black locust limbs. We had a sales tactic that was foolproof—especially because we didn't want to spend more than two or three hours at the market. Upon our arrival (any open space around the market perimeter was fair game in those days), the kids checked the prices of our competitors. Then we marked our produce slightly lower. We always sold out quickly. We had the most fun selling popcorn on the cob. One year we had several bushels of the cobs, some as long as six inches, some as short as two. We sold the ears three for twenty-five cents, pick the three you want. Of course everyone selected the largest three ears, right down to the last few scrawny cobs in the bottom of the bushel basket. Each customer thought he was buying the three largest cobs—and I suppose he was.

In the mid-1970s we moved our garden to an acre-and-a-half field southwest of the farmstead, on a little hill and next to a row of old white pines. The soil was considerably richer here and less dependent on regular rainfall. By this time my mother and father had moved off the home farm to live in Wild Rose, and I worked out an agreement with my dad; he would garden about a half acre of the plot, and we'd do the rest. Dad kept his plot at our farm for about ten years. It was a tangible way for him to keep his connection to the land, and he never missed a year. Gardening at our farm gave him some time with his grandchildren, in an environment where he was totally at home, working the soil. By the time he reached his late seventies, he continued to garden at his and my mother's house in Wild Rose but left the big garden at the farm to me. One way I kept track of Dad's health was to note the size of his garden each spring. He died in July 1993, but he had planted that spring: a few rows of radishes, lettuce, beans, and potatoes—a tiny plot compared to what he once tended.

Our garden soil is sandy and acidic, perfect for potatoes.

With our new garden space we had a new problem: deer. The deer population had steadily increased in the area, becoming a menace for anyone with a garden. Deer love gardens. They will eat vegetable crops before the best prairie grass, and they seem to prefer garden crops over farmers' corn or soybeans. By the middle 1970s we had herds of deer roaming our farm. Each spring a new crop of fawns emerged, and it seemed that every doe had twins. And every deer family found our garden, chewing the green bean plants to the ground, nipping off the corn, eliminating the peas, destroying the squash and pumpkin plants.

"Only thing to do is put up a ten-foot woven-wire fence. Best way to keep them out," a neighbor advised. I didn't want to erect a huge fence, and the cost would be well beyond my garden budget.

I heard other suggestions. "Plant more garden, so you have some left after the deer are finished." I didn't want a ten-acre garden, which is how much acreage I would have needed to keep the deer happy.

One suggestion made some sense: "Put a single-wire fence around the garden, buy some mothballs, put two or three in little mesh bags, and tie them to the fence. Space the bags a few feet apart, and you'll have no more problems." The theory seemed sound. Deer would catch a whiff of naphtha and leave our garden alone.

I believe the opposite proved true. Deer smelled the mothball bags from a great distance, and when they did, they knew a garden was near. They followed their noses to my garden. The mothballs attracted rather than repelled deer.

My brother Don, the barber, said, "Human hair in little bags on your fence will keep the deer away." Sounded plausible; a deer approaching the garden would catch human scent and rapidly beat a retreat. But not our deer. They like people, especially the gardens people plant.

Finally, I found a solution: a battery-powered electric fence. I know, some will say an electric fence is cruel to animals—but no more than a farmer using an electric fence to keep his livestock confined to their pasture. Our electric fence gives just enough of a jolt to dissuade a hungry deer from feasting on our crops. We learned that an electric fence need be only about three feet from the ground, because most deer walk while feeding, and they confront the fence with their chests. Deer are also quite smart. One encounter with the fence, maybe two, and they don't bother it again. A few years later we added a second wire, about a foot from the ground, which keeps the groundhogs, raccoons, and turkeys (who have enormous appetites) out of the garden, mostly.

We are now on our fourth garden spot, a tiny space compared to our early efforts but still quite large, maybe a quarter acre. Our present garden is just east of the cabin, in what was Weston Coombes's barnyard and pigpen fifty years ago.

Our earlier garden spots were too far from the well for irrigation, but now we can water the garden during dry spells. And nearly every growing season has one or more periods of no rain. We've also struck on a soil-enhancement tactic that has worked well. Each fall, after the potatoes are dug, the squash and pumpkins picked, the sweet corn stalks cut, the last of the rutabagas, onions, beets, and carrots harvested, I remove the fence and then hitch the tractor to the disk harrow and work into the soil the remnants of the garden. Then I plant winter rye, which comes up in a few days and provides a green cover for the garden, a protective blanket from the wind and a feed source for the deer and wild turkeys. Now the wild critters have easy access.

In the spring, when the frost is out of the ground and the soil is dry enough to be worked, I hitch my tractor to my plow and turn over the rye. The old agriculture books called this green manuring: plowing a green crop to provide organic matter to the soil.

Since my Wisconsin-based grandsons have gotten old enough to help, they're part of a garden planting and harvesting ritual here at the farm. Each spring Ben helps me put up the electric fence. "It's got to be right, Grandpa," he says. Ben measures the distance between the insulators on each post so they are exactly the same distance apart before he fastens the wire to them—he is more careful about this than I would be. Josh plants the pumpkin seeds each spring. Both the boys, who have done these tasks for half a dozen years now, start asking me in early May when we will "fix up" the garden.

We enjoy fresh vegetables all summer long, from the first radishes in spring to baked squash in the fall. There is something about eating green beans picked an hour ago, or munching on leaf lettuce that is only minutes from the garden, that seems to add flavor. We also enjoy tomato soup, tomato juice, and salsa that Ruth prepares each summer from our tomato crop. We store and eat potatoes through most of the winter and keep squash until Christmastime most years. Josh and Ben have a ready supply of Halloween pumpkins from those that Josh plants each year. We haven't sold our produce for years, not since the children left home. I am content to give away any excess we have.

Why do I garden, when it is so easy to buy vegetables at the supermarket or even farm-fresh produce at a farmers' market or farm stand? For me gardening is a vital connection to my land and to my past. As long as I can remember I have gardened, back to when I was a little boy helping my mother in the big farm garden that provided our family with fresh vegetables in season and canned vegetables and fruits throughout the long winter months.

Gardening is more than an annual ritual, although that is certainly a part of my need to plant a garden each year. Working in the garden is a way to remain close to the soil, to smell it, feel it, get it under your fingernails, and appreciate that our lives and the lives of millions of others in the world depend on soil.

Gardening is like life itself. For me, the beginning of a new year is a time to look ahead with plans, hope, and anticipation. Some of my plans work out, many don't, and occasionally something unexpected happens and I'm pleased. So it is with gardening. When the seed catalogs begin arriving after the first of the year, I read them from cover to cover, looking for new varieties and fresh ideas. I make plans that come into focus with my seed order. Then I wait for planting weather, most years in mid-April if the soil is dry enough and warm enough to plant the cool-weather crops, like potatoes, radishes, lettuce, cabbage, broccoli, and onions. By mid-May I am planting the rest of the seeds: green beans, rutabagas, beets, and sweet corn. I usually wait

Our pumpkins become jack-o-lanterns for the grandchildren, and Ruth makes pumpkin pies.

until Memorial Day to set out my tomato plants; they'll freeze with just the prediction of a chilly night. Frost still comes to central Wisconsin in May four years out of five.

With the garden crops in the ground, I wait to see what happens. No two years are ever the same. I'm surprised with the success of a new sweet corn variety. I'm disappointed with the poor yield of cucumbers from a variety that I've planted for years. Tomatoes ripening two weeks early, pumpkins failing to turn orange before the first frost, squash growing so well that it climbs up the stalks of the sweet corn, beets that shrivel and die after a groundhog eats off most of the vegetation—all are a part of gardening.

My father worked in his garden six weeks before he died at age ninety-three. I hope I can do the same.

Karner blue butterfly

Chapter 22

∞∞∞∞∞∞∞∞∞∞∞∞∞∞

Prairie and Karner Blues

"To make a prairie it takes a clover and one bee,
One clover, and a bee,
And revery. The revery alone will do,
If bees are few."

EMILY DICKINSON

We began restoring our prairie by default. When we first acquired the farm from my dad in 1966, my two brothers and I owned the one hundred acres together. We decided that the big field above the hill to the south of the pond and stretching to the farm's southern border would be an ideal location for a cornfield. The field was about fifteen acres, less hilly than much of the farm, with slightly heavier soil and rocks only here and there. No plowman wants to hear of rocks, no matter whether he farms with horses or the fanciest new mechanized equipment. Rocks break plows, bend tillage equipment, and fray the nerves of farmers.

My brothers and I asked David Kolka, a farmer neighbor and former schoolmate, if he'd be interested in planting the field with corn. We struck a deal in which he would give us a portion of the crop as rent; we hoped to take in enough money from the corn sold to pay our land taxes. The first couple years the rains came regularly, and our corn crop was average.

We planted corn for several years in the late 1960s. But then in 1970 or 1971 a low-rainfall year came along—they seem to come regularly to sandy farms—and David's corn crop was a near failure. We knew he would not get back from the corn sale what he had put into the project—time, machine, seed, and fertilizer costs. Our return on the project was near nonexistent. We amicably agreed to grow no more corn at Roshara, except for a few rows of sweet corn in the garden.

When David quit growing corn in the big field, the next season the land became a mass of weeds—ragweed, lambs quarter, foxtail, quack grass, even some thistles in the hollows. As we looked across an expanse of corn stubble and thriving weeds, we wondered if we'd made

True to its name, butterfly weed attracts many species of butterflies.

the right decision to quit working this field. Ironically, that season ample rain fell and the weeds grew abundantly, some waist high. My brothers and I were busy with our young families and our careers and paid little attention to this weed field. As farmers we had grown up fighting weeds on the home farm. We cultivated to eliminate them; we hoed them, chopped them, cut them with a scythe. Whenever there was a slack time in other farmwork, we worked at controlling weeds. Now we had allowed acres of weeds to grow undisturbed, to thrive without threat of hoe or sickle. In this field at least, the weeds had won the battle. We wondered what Dad would think when he saw our field of weeds, enough to provide weed seed for the entire community.

After about five years, the grasses and wildflowers slowly returned and the weeds began disappearing. With my wildflower identification book in hand, I spotted butterfly weed, two kinds of goldenrod, milkweed in profusion, and hillsides covered with brilliant blue blazing star.

In addition to the wildflowers, such native grasses as prairie June grass and little bluestem began appearing. I noticed an increase in butterflies flitting about, especially Monarchs, which are attracted to milkweed. A host of smaller butterflies of various colors appeared in the prairie, drawn by the beautiful orange butterfly weed. Honeybees and bumblebees also worked the wildflowers when they were in bloom, searching for nectar. One day I found a badger den in the prairie, a big hole in the ground with brown dirt piled up in front of it. Anthills appeared, some of them two feet high and crawling with these busy little insects. Now, some thirty years after beginning our prairie restoration, the changes continue. A year ago I spotted a big patch of needle grass growing on a side hill and on top of another hill found purple prairie clover.

Watching the transformation of these acres back to something like they were when Tom Stewart first broke the land here has been absolutely fascinating. Too often I hear from people

Goat's beard, one of nature's truly artistic creations

who want to develop a native prairie and are disappointed when it doesn't happen in a year or two. I've been observing my prairie develop for more than three decades, and the transformation continues. The joy of finding some new wildflower, grass, or butterfly is the payment I receive for my patience. The suspense of not knowing what I will discover next is part of the fun. Here I really have let nature take its course; I have planted no seeds, so whatever I find growing has gotten its beginning in some other way.

I have done little in the way of management in the prairie, except to cut rogue Scotch pine and box elder trees that appeared here and there. I had planned to do a periodic burn of my prairie, but both a DNR forester and a Federal Fish and Wildlife specialist advised against it because I have too many pines growing nearby. (Pines, of course, will burn like tinder.) So one April in the 1970s I hitched my rotary mower to the tractor and cut the dead and tangled grass. I've done this every few years since, and it has worked well, keeping volunteer trees and shrubs to a minimum and grinding up old grass and wildflower stems in preparation for a new season's growth.

ROSHARA'S PRAIRIE GRASSES

- **big bluestem** (*Andropogon gerardii*)
- **Indian grass** (*Sorghastrum nutans*)
- **little bluestem** (*Schizachyrium scoparium*)
- **needle grass** (*Stipa spartea*)
- **prairie June grass** (*Koeleria macrantha*)
- **purple love grass** (*Eragrostis spectabilis*)
- **switchgrass** (*Panicum virgatum*)

Prairie grasses in June

Starting in early spring, it seems there is something new growing or blooming in my prairie every week, right up to first frost, which usually comes in late September or early October. My laissez-faire approach to prairie restoration has been very effective, although it does take time. Nature, if given half a chance, tries to restore itself. I've found little bluestem grass and Indian grass in the prairie, and we have huge patches of purple love grass. I even have a sizable area of big bluestem grass that grows up to six feet tall on this poor land. What a treat to watch it grow each summer and produce seeds in the fall. Slowly the patch is becoming larger. Again, patience is the watchword.

I have lost my patience with the quack grass that has taken over a couple hollows in my prairie, crowding out everything else that might grow there. My next challenge is to battle this toughest of tough weedy grasses. I don't know how many hours my brothers and I spent hoeing quack grass out of the cucumber patch, the potato field, and even the hollows in the cornfields on our home farm. I suspect that long after I'm gone, country people will still cuss quack grass and debate how to get rid of it. I'm going to try once more, although ultimately I know I will fail. Quack grass has been winning for years. It will prevail.

In one of my many hikes around our newly acquired farm in 1966, I saw a carpet of purple flowers, some lighter in color, some darker, but all delicate and beautiful, on the south side of the property. This small patch of lupines (*Lupinus perennis*), about twenty or thirty feet square, grew in a little sandy, grass-free area that was exposed to full sun most of the day. It was mid-June, and the lupines were in full bloom.

On the farm where I grew up, just two miles north, I had never seen a lupine. So I knew our little patch was special. Little did I know then how special these lupines are.

In 1967 I devoted one of my newspaper columns to our lupine patch. I did some research on lupines and discovered some interesting facts. The word *lupine* (genus *Lupinus*) comes from *lupus*, the Latin name for wolf. When wolves were much more common, they were known to steal livestock from farmers. These same farmers thought that the tall, thick-growing purple-flowered plant stole nutrients from their soil, and thus they called it lupine.

While a wolf may on occasion steal a pig or a lamb from a farmer, the lupine does not steal from the soil. The opposite is true. Lupines are part of the large family of legumes (Leguminosae or Fabaceae), which also includes beans, peas, clover, and alfalfa. Legumes improve the soil thanks to nodules (little bumps) on the roots. Legumes contain bacteria that convert nitrogen in the soil into a form plants can use to grow.

Lupine

Lupines do have a dark side, however; like their cousins the peas, lupines have pods with seeds, but lupine seeds are poisonous to humans and animals. The lupine seed has a high alkaloid content, and foraging deer and other plant eaters know to avoid them.

In 1967 I noticed that several self-seeded Scotch pine trees had grown in and around the lupine patch. The next fall I cut them down. The next summer, the lupine patch expanded into the new available space. Clearly these wildflowers like full sun and little competition from other plants.

For years we did nothing with the lupines other than to keep trees from growing where the lupines grew. Each June we enjoyed the flowers and talked about their history. Then, in the mid-1990s, Jim Christensen, a friend who worked for the Wisconsin Department of Natural Resources, asked me if lupines grow on our farm.

"Yes, we have a small patch," I told him. The lupine area had grown to about an acre by this time.

"Do you have Karner blue butterflies?" Jim asked.

"What are they?" I responded. The look on Jim's face suggested I should know something about Karner blue butterflies (*Lycaeides melissa samuelis Nabakov*). He told me that the Karner blue is a federally endangered butterfly that lives only where lupines grow—and he said he thought I probably had some on my farm.

He described them: small, about the size of a postage stamp. The males have dark blue wings on top. On females the blue on the wings is less intense. Both males and females have black spots on the underside of their wings, with orange crescents and a black ring around the edges.

"Nope. I see lots of butterflies, but none like you describe," I said.

"You just haven't noticed them," Jim said, smiling.

"Maybe so," I said. "But I tend to notice things, especially at the farm."

"Would you mind if one of our biologists and I came up to your place for a visit in June, to see if we might spot some Karner blues?"

"Sure, love to have you. But I don't think we have any." I was intrigued by the possibility, though. Imagine having a federally endangered creature living on my farm.

A couple weeks later, in mid-June, Jim Christensen and Dave Lentz, who had a title several times larger than the butterfly (Karner Blue Habitat Conservation Plan Implementation Coordinator, Bureau of Forestry), arrived at the farm. I hiked them out to the lupine patch, where the flowers were in full bloom. It was a sight to see, Karner blue butterflies or no.

As we hiked, Dave asked me what I knew about Karner blues. I fessed up that until recently I'd never heard of the endangered insect. He told me that they had once been found in Michigan, Illinois, Indiana, Minnesota, Ohio, New Hampshire, and New York—and of course in Wisconsin, especially in the central sands area of the state. But now they were mostly extinct in some of these states, with the largest populations remaining in Michigan and Wisconsin. Karner blues especially liked places just like my farm that are hospitable to lupines. I nodded my understanding, but I was thinking, if they liked places like my farm, why hadn't I seen one?

We paused in the shade of an oak tree on the edge of the lupine patch, and Dave told me more about Karner blues. He'd found a blank slate who appeared interested.

"Do you know how these little butterflies reproduce?" Dave asked.

"No," I answered. By this time I knew Dave was going to tell me no matter what my answer.

He explained that without lupines there would be no Karner blue reproduction. Now I was curious.

"The little butterflies lay eggs on the lupine plants just about now," Dave said. The eggs remain on the plants throughout the rest of the summer and through the winter, hatching in late April of the following year, before the plants have flowered. The larvae, tiny caterpillars only a few millimeters long, crawl up on the lupine plants and eat the leaves. And that's *all* they will eat.

Karner blue butterfly

While Dave was talking I was sending my brain back to my college days, trying to remember how many millimeters made an inch. Somewhere deep down and far away I remembered that one inch equals about twenty-five millimeters. So these caterpillars were *really* small. I kept listening with a serious look on my face.

Dave told me, "There are two waves of Karner blues each summer." The caterpillars feed on the lupine leaves for three or four weeks and then form a chrysalis. The little butterflies emerge eight to ten days later. By mid-May the butterflies are flying around, sucking nectar from whatever wildflowers are available and searching for a mate. An individual adult lives for only five days or so. Once mating takes places, the females lay their eggs on lupine plants. A second brood hatches in late June to mid-July. The caterpillars feed on the lupine leaves and become butterflies in time to lay eggs in late summer.

What happened next fits within the category of life's embarrassing moments. We had barely stepped into the lupine patch when Dave spotted a Karner blue. He showed it to me. I wanted to say that I had seen these butterflies all along, for years, but had thought they were the

Eastern tailed-blue butterfly

kind that resulted in cabbage worms that fed on my garden. But for once I knew to keep my mouth shut. To mistake a famous federally endangered butterfly for a lowly cabbage worm was the ultimate in biological naïveté.

That fall Steve and I got out the chainsaw and clear-cut about three more acres of rogue Scotch pine from the eastern section of my prairie restoration in hopes that the lupine patch would spread and enlarge our home for the little Karner blues. Within three years, the sandy hillside where we cut the trees was covered with lupines—purple, white, deep purple, some tinged with pink. The Karner blue population expanded as well. Steve and I also discovered that the Karner blue butterfly is easily confused with other little blue butterflies that flit about our farm in early spring, especially the spring azure and the Eastern tailed-blue, both of which are similar in size and color to the Karner blue.

Karner blue butterflies are endangered or extinct in many places where they once lived. But not at Roshara. Our lupine/Karner blue restoration project is the most successful part of our entire prairie restoration. And it required little to accomplish. It took a little study, some advice and information from experts, a little tree cutting, and some patience. We have planted not one lupine plant nor collected and planted any lupine seeds. Once we removed the Scotch pines, the lupines spread on their own. The Karner blue butterflies followed.

The lupine patch has become one of our favorite places on the farm. When the lupines are in full bloom, they are a sight to behold: a sea of shimmering blue, with the occasional Karner blue butterfly adding a bit of intrigue to the mix. In many ways this part of my prairie restoration has been the most satisfying, seeing the lupines expand from a tiny plot to several acres and then discovering that we have these beautiful and very special butterflies. I sometimes think back to when Tom Stewart homesteaded this place in 1867 and wonder whether he saw lupines and Karner blues. I'm betting that he did.

WILDFLOWERS AT ROSHARA

BLUE/PURPLE

+ **bird's-foot violet** (*Viola pedata*), Violet family
+ **harebell** (*Campanula rotundifolia*), Bellflower family
+ **leadplant** (*Amorpha canescens*), Pea family
+ **Ohio spiderwort** (*Tradescantia ohiensis*), Dayflower family
+ **pasqueflower** (*Pulsatilla nuttalliana*), Buttercup family
+ **purple prairie clover** (*Dalea purpurea*), Pea family
+ **rough blazing star** (*Liatris aspera*), Aster family
+ **Russian vetch** (*Vicia villosa*), Pea family

+ **smooth aster** (*Aster laevis*), several varieties
+ **wild bergamot** (*Monarda fistulosa*), Mint family
+ **wild lupine** (*Lupinus perennis*), Pea family

PINK

+ **beardtongue** (*Penstemon grandiflorus*), Figwort family
+ **columbine** (*Aquilegia canadensis*), Buttercup family
+ **common milkweed** (*Asclepias syriaca*), Milkweed family

(continued on following page)

Russian vetch

+ **dotted mint** (spotted bee balm) (*Monarda punctata*), Mint family
+ **downy phlox** (*Phlox pilosa*), Phlox family
+ **joe-pye weed** (*Eupatorium maculatum*), Aster family
+ **pasture rose** (*Rosa carolina*), Rose family
+ **wild geranium** (*Geranium maculatum*), Geranium family

RED AND ORANGE
+ **butterfly weed** (*Asclepias tuberosa*), Milkweed family
+ **cardinal flower** (*Lobelia cardinalis*), Bellflower family
+ **orange hawkweed** (*Hieracium aurantiacum*), Aster family

YELLOW
+ **black-eyed Susan** (*Rudbeckia hirta*), Aster family
+ **butter-and-eggs** (*Linaria vulgaris*), Snapdragon family
+ **common mullein** (*Verbascum thapsus*), Snapdragon family
+ **early goldenrod** (*Solidago juncea*), Aster family
+ **hairy puccoon** (*Lithospermum caroliniense*), Borage family

+ **long-bearded hawkweed** (yellow hawkweed) (*Hieracium longipilum*), Aster family
+ **meadow goat's beard** (*Tragopogon dubius*), Aster family
+ **rough puccoon** (hoary puccoon) (*Lithospermum canescens*), Borage family
+ **showy goldenrod** (*Solidago speciosa*), Aster family

WHITE
+ **blackcap raspberry** (*Rubus occidentalis*), Rose family
+ **common dewberry** (*Rubus flagellaris*), Rose family
+ **daisy fleabane** (*Erigeron strigosus*), Aster family
+ **false Solomon's seal** (*Smilacina racemosa*), Lily family
+ **pussytoes** (*Antennaria neglecta*), Aster family
+ **Solomon's seal** (*Polygonatum biflorum*), Lily family
+ **white woodland aster** (*Aster divaricatus*), Aster family
+ **wild strawberry** (*Fragaria virginiana*), Rose family
+ **yarrow** (*Achillea millefolium*), Aster family

Chapter 23

◇◇◇◇◇◇◇◇◇◇◇◇◇◇◇◇◇◇◇◇

Forestry

"Those are too little, Grandpa. We want those big trees to be ours."
CHRISTIAN AND NICHOLAS APPS, AGES FIVE AND THREE

The results of thinning the pine plantation. Loggers piled the wood before hauling it to area paper mills.

My two brothers and I began planting trees at Roshara in the spring of 1966, before we had done much of anything else at the farm. We ordered one thousand red pine seedlings from the state tree nursery in Wisconsin Rapids; they arrived in mid-April. These seedling red pines, sometimes called Norway pine, were six to eight inches tall and bundled in bunches of twenty-five.

Following World War II, tree farmers in much of Waushara County had planted Christmas trees by the hundreds of thousands (the Wisconsin Christmas Tree Producers Association was formed in 1954). They planted mostly Scotch pine with the intention of shearing them (cutting off some new growth each summer). Without shearing, Scotch pine is not especially attractive, with branches spaced quite far apart. But the sheared trees grow thick and form perfect, pyramidal trees—the standard for how people used to think a Christmas tree should look.

Scotch pines grow fast, especially on sandy soils where there is little or no competition from grasses. Within eight or ten years, a Christmas tree farmer had a crop to sell. Waushara County Christmas trees were sold throughout the United States, and even today Wautoma, the county seat, prides itself on being the Christmas Tree Capital of the World.

Scotch pine seeds escaped from those Christmas tree plantations, and Scotch pines planted themselves in many places, including my farm, where they grew wild, essentially as weed trees. Other than sheared Christmas trees, Scotch pines are not particularly valuable (although I recently learned that they do have value for paper pulp). And many Scotch pines die young, at age twenty or thirty. A fungal disease attacks their root system, and it's not unusual to see them blown over by the wind, a hulk of dead and dying needles and branches.

When we bought our farm, several people asked me if we planned to plant the open fields with Christmas trees. "Make some money off those sandy acres," a neighbor said. I replied that we wanted to leave the old fields open and didn't want acres of Christmas trees. It was a wise decision. In the early 2000s the Christmas tree market, especially the demand for sheared Scotch pine, started to decline. Those who still buy live trees seem to prefer the more elegant Fraser fir, which is a slow grower, but a beautiful tree.

Red pines grow rapidly, are long-lived and beautiful, and when mature have considerable economic value. The paper mills like them; so do the log cabin sawmills. Mature trees are also suitable for sawed lumber.

Seedlings are planted in mid- to late April, when the frost is out of the ground, the soil moisture is high, and the seedlings are still dormant. The sooner after receiving the nursery stock, the better it is to plant them. We planted our first thousand red pines in four rows around our

Balsam fir seedling

farm boundaries. Every bit of our tree planting project was hard work. We hitched a one-bottom walking plow to Dad's Farmall H tractor, and with my brother Donald's and Dad's help I plowed four furrows along the front boundary of the farm and four more along the south boundary. I walked slowly behind the plow, holding the handles and recalling what it had been like when I used this same plow, but with a team of horses providing the power.

Planting the trees in furrows would give the little red pines an early advantage against grass competition. The open furrows would also capture and retain moisture when it rained. With the furrows made, we worked in two-person teams, Ruth and me, my Dad and Donald (the kids, still tykes at the time, also "helped"). One person walked backward, making a slit in the bottom of the furrow with a shovel. The second person, carrying fifty or so trees in a bucket of water, selected a tree and stuck it in the slit, making sure all the little roots were in the hole. The first person pushed the slit shut with his foot, removing all the air and forcing the soft, sandy soil around the tree's roots; then he or she backed up six feet and made another slit. The process continued. We planted rows of trees about eight feet apart, little tree after little

Heavy rains have cut deep gullies at several places on the farm.

tree, until it was time for lunch and the discovery that earning a living teaching didn't harden the muscles needed for tree planting. By suppertime I could scarcely move, and we had another five hundred trees to plant the next day.

We planted one thousand trees in 1967 and the same number in 1968. When we finished planting all around the property, we planted a few hundred on each of three steep side hills. All three hills were prone to washing (soil erosion); two of them already had gullies, where we planted more trees. Some years we planted in sunshine, others in rain, and once or twice we planted while it snowed. When the trees arrived, we planted them no matter the weather. We actually got some of the best survival rates from trees we planted in inclement weather, because the little roots never had an opportunity to dry.

After 1969 we reduced our tree planting to about fifty trees a year, sometimes fewer as we turned our attention to prairie restoration. By the early 1970s the first trees were far above the plowed furrows and doing well. Once the trees grew above the competition, mostly grass, they grew as much as three feet a year. Spring rains following the planting were the key to their survival.

Over the years we did nothing with the trees we planted. Once or twice the power company came along and topped some of those that were threatening the power line near the road, but otherwise we did no trimming or shearing.

Another field at Roshara, one that started at the dirt road that trailed by the farm and stretched west for several hundred yards up to a white pine windbreak, had been a cornfield only a year or two before Dad bought the place. We did nothing with this field except watch it turn from cornfield into a white pine plantation, seeded by the old pines that earlier farmers on this land had planted to stop Roshara's fields from blowing away during the dry and awful years of the Great Depression. I didn't pay much attention to these acres as the trees poked up above the weeds and grass and slowly took over, crowding out the vegetative competition as a grove of pine trees will do. By the time the trees were knee high and higher, we decided to leave them alone, to see what nature had in mind for this former cornfield. I was amazed at what happened. These self-seeded white pine trees became a forest, without any assistance from us whatever. Nature works in interesting ways if given an opportunity and some time.

In 2003 we signed up for the Managed Forest Lands Stewardship Forestry Plan, administered by the Wisconsin Department of Natural Resources. I was required to submit a detailed management plan for our farm's trees, which included thinning, cutting out Scotch pine, and replanting, all over a period of twenty-five years. In return I would receive a reduction in property taxes on my forested land—which is the majority of the farm.

Thinning the red pines we planted starting in 1966 was high on the agenda of work to be done. Six by eight feet had seemed an adequate distance to space the trees when we planted the seedlings, but now the branches were rubbing against each other. Some of the red pines were forty feet tall and two feet in diameter; those in more crowded growing situations were smaller. The trees were obviously crowded and not happy.

We hired a professional forester, T. D. Haukereid from Sun Prairie, to mark the trees for cutting and to prepare a bid list so that loggers in the area could offer bids to cut our trees. A strange sight it was: here, there, and everywhere, trees wearing bands of blue paint.

Wild Scotch pine covered parts of three side hills, and we decided to clear-cut them as well. As it turned out, most of these Scotch were large enough that we could sell them for pulpwood along with the red pine.

The white pine trees in the windbreak that John Coombes had planted when he owned the farm had conveniently cast their seeds to the east, and what had been a cornfield when we bought the place in 1966 was now a naturally growing white pine plantation, "thicker than the hairs on a dog," as the forester said. We decided thinning the white pine plantation was in order. The largest white pines would go for saw logs; the smaller ones we would add to the pulpwood pile.

Along the farm's northwest boundary, above the pond, several huge gullies had filled with naturally seeded quaking aspen trees, which we also cut for pulpwood. A small patch of black oak, maybe two or three acres, that grew on the far southwest side of the farm had been infected with oak wilt and were dying. "Cut them before they die," our forester said.

Back in the 1930s John Coombes had planted black locust trees to stop gullies from forming on a steep side hill not far from the pond. They did their job well, as black locusts grow fast, have a strong root system, and, with barbs an inch or more long, are left alone by tree-eating wildlife. In fact, the black locust trees had done far too well, climbing out of the gullies and marching along the hillside, crowding out almost all other vegetation with their competitive and thick-growing tendencies. Our Department of Natural Resources management plan said we should clear-cut the five-acre patch of locust trees and replant with another species, probably red pine. Rising natural and propane gas prices made the black locust valuable as stove wood.

Pine stump

The logging company that won our bid was Koerner Forest Products, Ltd., of Oshkosh, a big company that works in several counties and hires local cutters as subcontractors. The loggers arrived May 2, 2005, to begin cutting. For many decades, woodcutting meant wielding an ax, either a double-bit ax with two cutting edges, or a single-bit ax with one edge and a back end for hammering a wedge when things got dicey and the tree decided to pinch the crosscut saw. I was introduced to an ax when I was about twelve, and Dad didn't buy me a wimpy, lightweight boy's model with a short handle, either. He handed me one of the axes that we used to cut firewood for our woodstoves. Now, in 2005, the woodcutter came without an ax, without a crosscut saw, and without a chainsaw. One man with his machine was doing the work once done by three or four men, maybe more. He drove a monster machine, a huge Caterpillar-type beast with metal tracks twenty-two inches wide and twelve feet long officially known as a "FabTek FT 133 Tracked Boom Harvester with an eighteen-inch processor." According to the FabTek Company, their 133 model weighs 35,000 pounds, has a 165-horsepower diesel engine, and is computer controlled. Top speed is a little over two miles per hour. The "processor"

Logs await transport to a sawmill.

part of the machine is attached to a boom that can reach out more than twenty feet. The processor does the cutting and limbing, all controlled from within the machine's cab.

Like a creature from a science fiction movie, the huge machine crawled up to a tree. The arm with the processor at the end swung forward and grabbed the tree's trunk. A built-in chainsaw emerged and sliced off the tree. Immediately the arm tipped the tree horizontal, often crashing it into other trees. The processor cut off the limbs and sliced the tree into one-hundred-inch lengths—the standard size for pulpwood. The machine eased forward to the next tree, and the next, investing scarcely a minute per tree.

The machine cut larger-diameter trees, too, into varying lengths depending on the size of the tree. Some of the largest, those thirty and more inches in diameter, were sliced into ten-foot logs; those around twelve to fifteen inches in diameter, suitable for log cabin logs, were cut fourteen or sixteen feet in length. Many cabin builders in our region prefer cabins constructed of logs, and three log cabin sawmills operate within five miles of our farm, so we had a ready market for these logs nearby. The pulpwood in one-hundred-inch lengths would go to paper mills along the Wisconsin River (Wisconsin Rapids, Port Edwards) or on the Fox River (Neenah, Menasha, Kaukauna).

A second machine with one operator picked up the logs, piled them on its back, and hauled them to huge piles where they awaited a truck to transport them to the paper plants or sawmill. This machine, a FabTek 344 B, called a forwarder, ran on four rubber tires twenty-four inches wide and five feet tall, was powered by a 125-horsepower diesel engine, and weighed 24,500 pounds. Its boom could reach more than twenty-one feet to grab a log, lift it, and load it on the machine's back end.

We didn't arrive at the farm until four days after the start of cutting. Huge piles of logs greeted us on either side of the driveway. I walked up to where I heard the loggers working and snapped some photos of the machines in action. After a tour around the farm to see where they had cut, I came back to where they were both taking a break. I introduced myself, and we chatted for a bit. The cutter's name was Scott, a young fellow from Wild Rose with long black hair and a camouflage shirt. The hauler, Lyle, was an older man from near Redgranite with a big gray beard, sparkly eyes, and a Santa Claus shape. We talked about logging and pulp cutting and how it had changed over the years.

Our talk got around to the DNR and their many rules. "Can't cut any oaks from May 1 until fall," Lyle said. "Stupid rule. Something about spreading oak wilt disease. Ask them how hauling oak logs spreads oak wilt and they tell you they don't know. Damn rule is still there. Can't cut your oak until fall—missed the deadline by three days." I offered that I thought oak wilt spread by the roots of infected trees touching disease-free trees and giving them the fungus, and both men agreed.

I returned to the farm a few weeks later, and the cutting had progressed to the back of the farm, where the loggers were thinning red pines and aspen and poplar that had self-seeded. They had cut two side hills of Scotch pine. Some of the Scotch had reached heights of forty feet, but now the hillsides were bare, except for an occasional oak or white pine tree.

I surveyed the log piles: three in the yard near the buildings and a fourth in the old garden to the south, some white pine and some black locust. One pile of white pine logs had several trees twenty and more inches in diameter and ten feet long. Some of these trees were sixty and more years old. West of the white pine windbreak were more piles of white pine and red pine pulpwood. One pile was 10 feet high and 120 feet long. In the prairie above the gullies was a huge pile of Scotch pine and another of poplar. The processor takes off most of the poplar bark when it cuts off the limbs, producing a sweet smell quite different from the evergreen smell of the white and red pine.

The logger had clear-cut the black locust patch, resulting in pile of eight-foot-long black locust logs stretching out one hundred feet wide and twenty feet high.

I picked my way through the white pine plantation, stepping over scattered limbs. The smell of the Northwoods was everywhere. I could hear the engine roaring from the north side of the farm, above the pond, where the woodcutter was cutting poplars. There were deep gullies there—gullies that could gobble up the cutter's monster machine if he wasn't careful.

Rain started falling about six-thirty that cold, dreary May morning—a steady, penetrating rain that seeped into the ground without much runoff. About seven o'clock a huge red log transport truck from Koerner Forest Products appeared in my driveway. The driver headed up the logging road to the log piles south of the buildings and on top of a little hill. But here was

TREES AT ROSHARA

DECIDUOUS

+ American elm (*Ulmus americana*)
+ big tooth aspen (*Populus grandidentata*)
+ black cherry (*Prunus serotina*)
+ black locust (*Robinia pseudoacacia*)
+ black oak (*Quercus velutina*)
+ black willow (*Salix nigra*)
+ box elder (ashleaf maple) (*Acer negundo*)
+ bur oak (*Quercus macrocarpa*)
+ chokecherry (*Prunus virginiana*)
+ common honey locust (*Gleditsia triacanthos*)
+ cottonwood (*Populus deltoides*)
+ Kentucky coffee tree (*Gymnocladus dioica*)
+ paper birch (*Betula papyrifera*)
+ pin cherry (*Prunus pennsylvanica*)
+ quaking aspen (popple) (*Populus tremuloides*)
+ red maple (*Acer rubrum*)
+ tea crabapple (*Malus hupehensis*)

+ white oak (*Quercus alba*)
+ wild apple (*Pyrus malus*)
+ wild plum (*Prunus americana*)

CONIFEROUS

+ balsam fir (*Abies balsamea*)
+ European larch (*Larix decidua*)
+ Fraser fir (*Abies fraseri*)
+ jack pine (*Pinus banksiana*)
+ Norway spruce (*Picea abies*)
+ red cedar (*Juniperus virginiana*)
+ red pine (Norway pine) (*Pinus resinosa*)
+ Scotch pine (*Pinus sylvestris*)
+ white fir (*Abies concolor*)
+ white pine (*Pinus strobus*)
+ white spruce (*Picea glauca*)

In two or three years the trash left after a pine thinning will decompose and disappear.

one of the few places on the farm with clay soil, and the rain had turned the newly graded road into a sea of slippery mud.

I watched from the cabin window as the big semi jackknifed on the hill, and I wondered what words came from the cab as the truck roared and the wheels spun and the clay mud flew. Finally, after considerable jockeying, the driver backed the rig down the hill and out to the road, where he turned around and backed into my yard. He crawled onto the back of the truck, where he perched on a little pedestal to operate a boom that picked logs off the piles and stacked them on the truck.

About this time, the woodcutter gave up working in the driving rain, and he appeared in his pickup, driving slowly down the slippery hill that had hung up the log truck. The two men talked for a half hour or so, and then the cutter left in his pickup. (Apparently because of the rain, the forwarder driver hadn't come to the farm that day.) The truck driver returned to his pedestal standing high in the rain and loaded the remaining pulpwood from the pile in the driveway. Finally he left, and a great quiet returned to the farm, with only the sounds of a pleasant May rain dripping from the cabin's roof and the snapping and crackling of the pine wood in the cookstove.

The logger finished cutting about two weeks later, except for the black oak, which could not be cut until after September 1. Logging trucks hauled load after load of logs from the stacks scattered all around my farm. They had their problems; the hill just west of the old white pine windbreak is too soft and sandy to support a loaded logging truck. One truck sank into the sand, and the driver had to unload all the wood and call a colleague working nearby to pull him out. They hauled the unloaded wood up the hill with the forwarder and reloaded the semi. It took most of half a day. Of course, the hill was a rutted mess and will take a long time to heal.

That July I explored the area where the loggers had cut the Scotch pine. Little oak trees were appearing everywhere, self-seeded where Scotch pine had once dominated. The black locust stumps were sprouting beyond belief. I found a stump and measured it—twelve inches in diameter. Then I counted the new sprouts. I got to seventy-six, without counting the smallest, shortest ones. Several of the taller sprouts were already four feet, with spines that would tear skin and penetrate cowhide leather gloves.

In mid-October the loggers returned to cut the marked black oak trees that were suffering from oak wilt disease. This time just a single cutter came, working with a chainsaw, cutting the giant oaks one at a time. He notched the tree, cutting out a wedge of wood on one side of the trunk, and then went around to the other side and cut it off. The trees, some more than one hundred years old, crashed to the ground in a flurry of flying leaves and broken branches. The woodcutter then cut off the side branches and cut the trunk into eight-foot lengths for firewood.

I had resisted cutting these majestic oaks on the far west side of Roshara. They provided food and shelter for squirrels, ruffed grouse, wild turkeys, owls, songbirds, and raccoons. I enjoyed walking among them in spring when they were first leafing, in summer when it was several degrees cooler in their shade, in fall when their green leaves were turning to many shades of brown, and in winter when their naked branches thrust upward to slate gray skies. But my forester had shown me where the dreaded oak wilt disease had begun infesting my oaks— several were already dead and more were dying. So the oaks came down, some with trunks three feet across and solid wood throughout, others so hollow and diseased that only a thin layer of live wood surrounded a huge rotted-out space. And the logging trucks returned once more to haul the big logs off to mills, to be sliced into wood that would become fancy furniture, flooring, and other wooden products.

One day after the cutting was complete, Scott Koerner of Koerner Forest Products, Ltd., came out to the farm. We discussed how he planned to repair my field and forest trails that had been torn up by logging trucks and cutting equipment. Fixing the roads was part of the logging contract, so the question was not whether it would be done but how to do it to my satisfaction. We had a good discussion. How different this was from as recently as twenty years ago, when the loggers disappeared after the cutting was finished and the landowner had to repair his or her own roads.

We talked about how the logging business has changed in recent years. Scott, a young, serious fellow, said he still feels like the word *crook* is written across his forehead when he talks to some landowners. He and many other modern loggers, in concert with private and Department of Natural Resources foresters, have worked to change the image of loggers. "We're trying hard to be partners," with the landowner, Scott said. So far I've been pleased with our relationship.

In a couple of weeks Koerner had my field roads back in order. They graded the hills, filled in the little gullies that formed with the summer rains, and seeded the hillsides with rye to hold the soil in place. For the hill leading to the field south of the buildings, Koerner not only graded but made a diversion ditch that they filled with gravel to keep the rains from rushing down the rather steep hill. Along the woods road, they hauled in fill dirt to widen the road in several places where the logging trucks and logging equipment had smashed off the edges of the road.

~~~~~~

We also have a small family forest at Roshara, located on a little side hill just south of the buildings. It consists of trees planted for each member of our family. When we first bought the farm in 1966, we planted a little spruce tree for each of our children. These trees are now forty feet tall, their branches touching each other. We have trees for spouses and a tree for each of the five grandchildren, planted the year after each was born. When the grandchildren visit, one of the first things they want to see is "their" tree. When grandsons Christian and Nicholas were five and three, we hiked out to see their trees. "Those are too little, Grandpa. We want those big trees to be ours." Now their little trees, probably six or eight inches tall when we planted them, are three and four feet tall.

In 1972 or 1973, when we were staying at a cabin at Lake George near Rhinelander, Sue got permission to take a tiny balsam fir tree home with her. She was ten or eleven at the time. We planted the tree near the pump house, and for many years it was the only balsam fir on the farm. Since then I have planted fifty more because Sue's tree, which is not supposed to grow on our sandy, droughty soil, is now forty feet tall and growing taller every year.

Our forestry work has provided much enjoyment for our entire family. It has also been essentially our only source of farm income—we sold a total of forty-three double semi loads of logs in our 2005 logging operation. However, the value of planting and caring for trees goes well beyond the monetary, as we discovered early on. Someone recently asked me, when he heard I was about to plant several thousand more trees, "Why, at your age, are you planting trees that you will never see mature?"

"My grandchildren will," I answered.

Our forest-management activities take up a good deal of time at the farm, but it is a fun time for me—mostly. My biggest challenge these days is managing the rampaging black locusts that seem intent on taking over the farm. In addition to mowing my prairie every couple of years, I mow four other little fields (about five or six acres total) every year to slow the black locust encroachment. A black locust tree will grow four feet in a season, but by cutting them off each year, I keep them in check.

On the upside, mowing these little fields gives me a chance to drive my John Deere tractor with the rotary mower and see what I am accomplishing immediately as black locust trees are ground into oblivion. My DNR forest-management plan gives me direction and suggestions for my forestry activities, but it doesn't tell me how to rid the place of the miserable black locust.

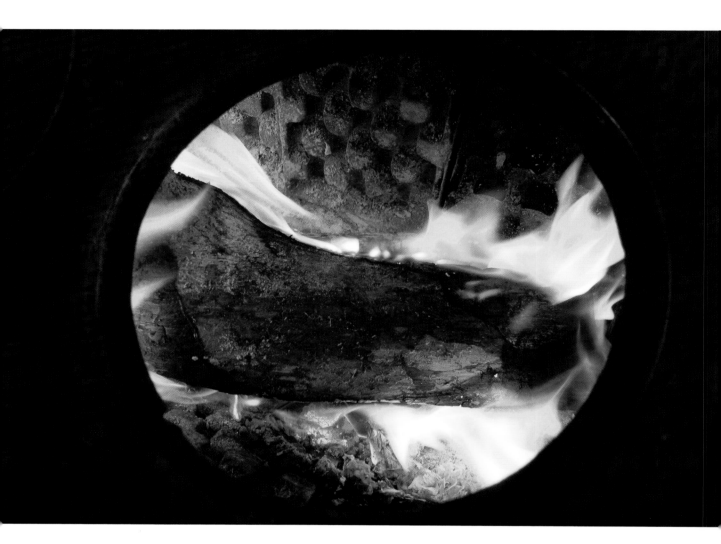

The cabin's wood-burning cookstove cooks meals and heats much of the building.

Chapter 24

⋄⋄⋄⋄⋄⋄⋄⋄⋄⋄⋄⋄⋄⋄⋄⋄⋄⋄⋄

Making Wood

"Reading a block of wood is like reading a person, trying to find out what that person believes and values, whether he or she is truthful, is hiding something, or is open and gets right to the point."

STEVE APPS

Making wood is a country term that baffles young people today. Trees make wood, don't they? People don't make wood! But they do. Anybody who has had any experience with woodstoves knows what making wood is about. I grew up with woodstoves; two of them heated our old drafty farmhouse, another kept the pump house above freezing, and a fourth kept the potato cellar above thirty-two degrees while the potatoes waited for market.

Two woodstoves keep our cabin at Roshara comfortably warm during the long winter months. The cookstove in the kitchen not only keeps the cabin reasonably warm by itself, it also doubles as a place to cook meals. I light the backroom stove only when the temperature hangs around zero most of the day and slides well below at night. These two stoves burn considerable wood, and thus making wood continues to be a yearly ritual at the farm. At one time or another the entire family is involved in the process.

For me the best and most pleasant time to start making wood is a cool day in late October or early November, when the smells of fall still permeate the air. When I was a kid, making wood meant axes and crosscut saws. Today, my STIHL chainsaw does most of the cutting. The crosscut saw has been relegated to antique status, and I use my ax only to help solve problems, as when the chainsaw becomes hung up and the blade won't move.

My son Steve and I have been in charge of the cutting part of making wood for the past several years. We can usually cut enough wood for the winter season in one day, with another day relegated to splitting and piling.

Bacon fries in a cast-iron skillet on the cookstove.

We prefer oak wood for firewood, although a couple of seasons we burned black cherry until a friend pointed out that black cherry had considerable value for lumber—we were allowing good money to go up in smoke. I also burned black locust for two or three years in our woodstoves at Roshara. The wood is hard, and it burns hot and holds the heat, but I couldn't get past the aroma, which to me smelled a lot like horse manure. I burn some pine wood, but mostly for kindling to get an oak fire started.

The first step in making wood is to find a tree suitable for cutting, usually one that has already died. Felling a tree is an art. The biggest challenge is to avoid having the tree you cut get "hung up"—caught in another tree on its way to the ground. Every year several woodcutters in Wisconsin are killed from hung-up trees that fall unexpectedly during the cutting process. So we take our time, walking around the tree to figure out its natural lean and looking for trees growing too near. Then the sawing begins. I set the choke on the saw and pull the rope starter a couple times. If I'm lucky, the saw starts. Sometimes the beast sputters and fusses and I cuss a bit before it finally fires and the chain begins turning. I wear a helmet that includes sound-cutting muffs, a metal screen in front of my face, and a hard plastic surface to ward off small limbs striking me while I work. With the saw turning at full speed, I cut a notch in the tree in the direction I want it to fall; then on the side opposite the notch I saw through the tree, watching all the while that the tree indeed plans to fall where I think it should. With a loud crack, the tree begins to topple. I yell, "Timber," the classic call in the woods alerting all creatures to stay clear, and the tree crashes to the ground in a cloud of broken limbs and falling leaves. With the tree down, I saw off the limbs and stack them in piles for wildlife homes—a place for rabbits and ruffed grouse to find shelter. Steve and I saw the wood into stove-length blocks, toss them on the trailer, and haul them to the pump house/ woodshed. Once we've got the wood unloaded, the real work begins: The oak blocks, which depending on the size of the tree might measure two to three feet in diameter, must be split into woodstove-size pieces.

Splitting mauls are our tools of choice, weighing from six to eight pounds or more. Splitting wood requires more than brute strength, but extra strength is certainly an asset. Good eye-hand coordination is a must as well. It takes considerable experience to strike a block of oak wood in the exact place you want.

But more than all that, the ability to read the wood—clearly an art form—comes into play. Steve is six foot three and weighs something over two hundred pounds; he has the strength and the long arms that help in splitting wood. He also subscribes fully to the concept of "reading the wood." And he goes even further. Steve says, "Reading a block of wood is like reading a person, trying to find out what that person believes and values, whether he or she is truthful, is hiding something, or is open and gets right to the point. Blocks of wood are like that. You've got to study each one carefully before you swing the heavy maul. What's hidden inside the block? An ornery knot that will stop the maul cold or a straight grain that is easily split?" Steve places each block to be split on a white oak splitting block, walks around the block and studies it, and then with a mighty swing brings the maul down hard. Most of the time the block pops open. But not always.

"Making wood" for the two cabin wood stoves is an annual October task.

"Same with people," Steve says. "You think you've got somebody figured out, but you haven't."

Occasionally, every hundred blocks or so, Steve gives up on one. "Just like people. Some you just can't get along with, no matter what."

Once the wood is split—I must confess that I do far less splitting than I once did—we pile the wood on the ground outside the pump house/woodshed to dry over winter. Even with lots of snow, winter's low humidity makes it a good time for drying wood.

When spring rolls around and much of the woodpile in the shed is depleted, we move the wood from outside the pump house to inside—another family project. Grandsons Josh and Ben; daughter Sue, her friend Paul, and his son, Joel; and Steve and his partner, Natasha, have all helped. We pass the sticks of stovewood from person to person until the tall pile

We dry split wood for a year before burning it in the cabin stoves.

outside is no pile at all, and the empty space inside the pump house/woodshed is now filled and ready for the following fall's heating season. The wood will continue drying inside throughout the summer. By fall there is no sputtering and excess smoking when the wood is fed to the cookstove, and there is less danger from chimney fires, too, as the dry wood burns more completely with little or no residue left to accumulate in the chimney.

The only chore left is carrying the wood to the wood box next to the cookstove—a several-times-a-day task during cold winter days. There's a saying that those who cut wood are twice warmed—once during the cutting and again with the burning. The person who wrote those words must not have known about all the *other* opportunities for warming, from the time that the tree is cut to when the wood is piled in the wood box.

With all the more modern ways to heat one's home these days, there is still something to be said for seeing the flames, smelling the smoke from the chimney, and hearing the crackling and snapping of wood as the flames consume it. Burning wood is a primitive, ancient experience. It's important to occasionally be reminded of these fundamental and primitive things.

Chapter 25

Deer Hunting

"The hunt is up, the morn is bright and grey,
The fields are fragrant and the woods are green."
WILLIAM SHAKESPEARE

Sunset, hunting season

Five fifteen A.M. The Big Ben windup alarm clock clangs loudly. I crawl out of bed, stumble over to the window, and look at the thermometer—thirty degrees. I need to know the temperature to decide how many layers of clothes I will pull on. First comes the long underwear—two-piece style, not the old-fashioned type with the trapdoor in the back that I once wore in the winter. Next it's a heavy flannel shirt and two pairs of blue jeans and wool socks.

I go out to the kitchen, crumple up some newspaper, and stuff it in the wood cookstove. I stick in a piece of fire starter and a couple small pieces of oak and touch a match to the paper. Soon the stove begins to warm the chilly room. I plug in the coffeepot and begin rounding up my gear for the hunt—rifle, bullets, knife, hunting license.

Then I pull on more clothing: a down vest, a down jacket, my blaze orange jacket in size XXL to fit over everything, and my blaze orange cap with earflaps. Finally my boots—Sorels with rubber bottoms, leather tops, and felt liners. A bit of truth I learned a long time ago: Keep your head warm, keep your feet warm and dry, and keep your fingers warm. But where are my blaze orange gloves? I find them in the closet on the porch, where they've been stored for the long nonhunting season.

I fill the thermos with black coffee, grab my rifle and L.L. Bean folding chair (in camouflage color), and head out the back door of the cabin into the night, for it is still very much night at five forty-five on a late-November morning in central Wisconsin.

Four inches of snow fell a few days ago, so with a near-full moon I have no trouble following the trail to my deer stand, on the south shore of the pond. The day after the snow the temperature fell to five degrees, so the pond is frozen and snow covered. It looks like a big, white field in the moonlight. Snow hangs on the brush around the pond, and the thick grass, once near head-high, has been smashed flat by the heavy snow.

I find a flat place near the pond for my folding chair and sit down, scanning the east and west shores of the pond in moonlight. Daylight is supposed to come around six thirty, and that's when the hunting season officially begins. I zip the down jacket closer to my chin as I settle into my chair. It is my fifty-ninth consecutive year of deer hunting. Many friends of my vintage are sitting by a swimming pool in Florida or swinging a golf club in Arizona. They can't understand why I would get up before dawn on a cold morning, sit by a frozen pond in the dark, and wait for a buck to come by. On mornings like this, I sometimes have trouble understanding it myself. But deer hunting is a sacred event for some people—myself included. It is much more than shooting deer and bragging about the results.

Deer hunting is a time for reflection, and for testing one's patience.
The annual hunt is a family tradition at Roshara.

I started hunting with my dad when I was twelve, and as early as age nine or ten I was allowed to walk with him while he hunted. I learned early some of what is necessary. Keep quiet. No talking. Watch where you walk so you aren't cracking dead branches and otherwise making a racket as you walk through the woods. Stop often to listen and look. Learn the difference in sounds between a squirrel running on dead leaves and a deer walking through the woods. Learn to look for movement, a flash of brown, a glimpse of white. It is easier when snow is on the ground. A deer's brown coat contrasts well with the white. It is much more difficult to spot a deer on bare ground. Their camouflage is near perfect.

Above all, learn to be patient—to stand or sit without moving for long periods of time. After a half hour or so, the woods come alive when you do that. Birds reappear—in winter they include noisy and nosy chickadees that will come within a few feet to check on this strange creature. Juncos come out of hiding and continue eating. Woodpeckers resume their rat-a-tat pounding on dead trees. Sometimes you will spot a hawk, as I did this morning, circling the pond in a big sweep, calling, "Ka-ree, ka-ree." And then a real treat: a flock of white swans flies over, making a whistling sound as they retreat from their northern breeding grounds to a warmer climate.

Slowly, moonlight gives way to daylight. But I see no sign of the sun yet at seven, as it has to crawl above a line of trees to the southeast. I pull the zipper on my down jacket a little tighter to my chin and shift my rifle on my lap.

I carry a 30–30 Winchester model 94 rifle. It's a lever action, the kind you often see in the old Western movies. At one time it was the deer rifle of choice for most hunters. According to its serial number it was made in 1951, so it's had lots of experience. I bought it from a friend who was ill. It was near new, and I paid thirty dollars for it. My friends accused me of taking advantage of a sick friend. But he said he needed the money more than he needed the rifle.

Today, in our hunting party, the 30–06 is a more likely caliber for a deer rifle. It shoots a bit farther than a 30–30, has more powder in its bullets, and thus sends the bullets along faster than my rifle does. But I still swear by my old Winchester 94. Some call it a brush gun, which means you can hunt in deep woods and the bullet won't be deflected by a small tree or a tag elder or other things that may be in the way of the bullet. Some of the bigger-caliber rifles have more power, but with more power the bullet is more likely to deflect if it hits something in its path.

My son Steve, who also has been hunting since he was twelve, uses a 7mm deer rifle. It's a heavy gun, but it shoots a long distance—maybe twice as far as my 30–30 accurately shoots. He has an enormous scope on it as well—it's variable from about four power to fourteen power. Nobody, not even Steve, can hold a rifle steady when the scope is cranked up to fourteen power, so he uses a monopod, a one-legged stand, to hold his weapon steady.

About ten years ago I bought a scope for my Winchester. Up to that time I had been hunting with open sights—the kind where you line up a little groove on the back of the rifle with a tiny ball on the end of the barrel and the game that you hope to bag. Open sights are surely the old-fashioned way of hunting, but I finally gave in to using a scope. Mine goes from 1.5 power to 4.5 power. If the scope is sighted in properly, you have only to put the crosshairs you see in the scope on the point you want the bullet to hit and that's what happens—some of the time anyway. My Winchester has enough magnification so I can tell at a hundred yards whether a deer has antlers. It's also good for watching woodpeckers working, swans flying over, squirrels climbing trees, and hawks circling.

My father used a 30–30 Savage deer rifle. He never used a scope and never lacked in accuracy, either. He brought down a deer when he was in his early nineties, and with open sights. "They never steam up, never are covered with snow, have no crosshairs to worry about," he said.

My father gave me a hunting knife on my twelfth birthday, the year that I could legally go deer hunting. The knife was made by the Marble Company in Gladstone, Michigan. It has a fixed blade about six inches long, with a leather handle and a leather sheath. I took it to school that fall, to show the teacher and my friends, all of whom thought I was lucky to get such a fine birthday present.

The knife is a bit time worn, as it has field dressed many rabbits and squirrels, a ruffed grouse or two, a few pheasants, and several deer. When I was a kid, the meat of choice on our table in fall was wild game. As a kid I hunted often, and with purpose.

On my twelfth birthday I received this leather-handled hunting knife.

I glimpse a spot of brown to the left of where I'm sitting. Three deer come into view on the hillside to the west of the pond, in a little opening in the trees. I quickly bring up the rifle and look through the scope—no antlers. All females. Then I see the back end of a fourth deer. Its head is behind a tree. And then the four are gone, disappearing into the woods. A shot of adrenaline quickly warms me. I put the rifle back on my lap, pull down the zipper on my down jacket, and push up my cap.

I reach for my thermos and pour a cup of coffee, balancing the cup and my rifle on my lap as I screw tight the cover to keep the rest of the coffee warm. I sip the coffee, look off to where I saw the deer, glance all around the pond, and take another sip. What could be better than this?

I hear a loud woodpecker noise to my right and point my scope in the direction of the sound. A pileated woodpecker is pounding away on a dead poplar, its head moving like a jackhammer.

In the little field to the right of the pond I spot three more deer, all does, walking slowly. I glance at my watch. It is eight-thirty and the temperature has climbed little since before dawn. I pull up the zipper on my jacket again and sink back into my L.L. Bean stool—it has a canvas back and is quite comfortable.

Land use change has affected hunting dramatically in our community. Back in the 1950s and 1960s almost none of the farmers here posted their land with No Trespassing signs. This meant we could walk for miles in search of deer, and we did. Today none of the private land in our community is open to hunting, except by permission or through lease, which means you pay to hunt on a person's land. My brothers and I talk about those days, of the deer shot and the many that got away. But mostly we recollect walking through the woods in the fall, and through neighbors' fields, always being careful to keep a goodly distance from farm buildings and livestock. We hunted with our neighbors, as nearly all of them were deer hunters in those days. We organized hunting drives, where three or four of us would walk through a mile or two of woods, while our fellow hunters lined up along the edge of the woods hoping we'd scare something out. Sometimes we did; often we didn't.

But we don't hunt that way anymore. We stay on our own property, on my sixty-five acres plus my brother's thirty-five, and we respect the No Trespassing signs of our neighbors (some of whom we've never met, as they live in the city).

Why do I continue to hunt deer after all these years? I consider myself an environmentalist. I am a bird-watcher, a lover of wildlife, a builder of native prairies, and a protector of Karner blue butterflies. Why do I continue hunting deer? A blood sport, some call it. Barbaric, others say. "What gives you the right to kill another living creature?" thoughtful persons ask.

The answer is complicated and multilayered. I grew up on a farm in the midst of the Great Depression. During the winter months we ate wild game regularly, along with food from the garden and a hog we butchered in late fall. Hunting was as natural as harvesting potatoes. The purpose was to provide food. So I learned hunting skills well—how to stalk, how to listen, how to walk in the woods, and how to shoot straight. Dad drummed into us that if we killed something, it should be as quick and painless as possible, whether we were butchering a pig or shooting a squirrel. And if we killed something, we ate it. No question about it. In those days hunting was a necessity, another source of food. One of the reasons I continue hunting, I suspect, is a nod to my history, to my upbringing. When I was a kid nobody questioned hunting or owning and using a gun. I knew only one neighbor who didn't hunt and didn't believe in it. Floyd Jeffers was quiet about his beliefs, but he did not allow anyone to hunt on his land.

Hunting with my father taught me not only the skills for hunting but much about understanding, enjoying, and respecting nature. Most of the time spent hunting is spent sitting or walking in the woods and fields, looking and listening—and thinking. It's sitting quietly without phone, radio, TV, computer, or other interruption. Hunting is an opportunity for solitude that is difficult to find these days.

For many of us, hunting is tradition. The opening day is marked on our calendars every year months in advance. It is something that we are compelled to do, because we do it every year. It is a time to look for our hunting gear, reflect on earlier years, and feel good about the fact that we can still do it. We hunt deer because we have always hunted deer.

After my brothers and I left home, we always returned to the home farm for the opening day of deer season. It was a chance to be with our father, who loved walking in the woods and enjoyed swapping stories of earlier deer seasons. Later, Dad's grandsons—my two boys, Jeff and Steve, and my brother Don's three sons, Marc, Eric, and Matt—were with us on opening day. It was a grand family reunion. My mother understood all this, as did Don's wife. But my wife came from a nonhunting family, so the lure of opening day was not only a bit of a mystery to her, but a bemusement. As the years passed, she has joined in the family gathering for parts of the tradition, which include a big hunter's lunch at our cabin on opening day, when we all gather and share the morning's adventures, or lack thereof.

My father hunted until he was ninety-two. Since his passing in 1993, we carry on the family tradition. Last year my twelve-year-old grandson, Josh, hunted with me. He did not carry a gun, but he sat with me on my deer stand and saw a deer, too, much to his amazement. Josh is the fourth generation of our family who has hunted at Roshara.

PART IV

A Sense of Place

There is something mysterious about tree branches in winter.

Chapter 26

<><><><><><><><><><><><>

Solitude

"Keep close to Nature's heart . . . and break clear away, once in awhile, and climb a mountain or spend a week in the woods. Wash your spirit clean."

JOHN MUIR

Henry David Thoreau wrote, "I find it wholesome to be alone the greater part of time. To be in company, even with the best, is soon wearisome and dissipating. I have never found the companion that was so companionable as solitude." While I don't fully agree with Thoreau—it appears he would value solitude over conversation with others—I do need solitude in my life, and I find it at my farm. I enjoy being alone, I seek it out, and seldom if ever am I lonely when I am alone there.

For me, solitude is a way to escape the demands, requests, and pressures of everyday life. A way to run from the crowds who constantly push, literally and figuratively. Solitude is the road to finding the side of myself that is often buried and neglected—it allows me to come out from behind myself and blink in the light of the bright sun.

Being alone allows me to think uninterrupted, or to not think at all. It is important to allow my mind to go blank from time to time, without a need to produce, decide, consider, weigh, figure out, lament, or whatever other activity the mind does during the course of a typical day.

I find great joy in friends and friendship, in children and family, but I also value dearly my regular opportunities for solitude. Both are important to me in liberal doses, and one is not more important than the other. To be sure, being alone and being with others appear to be

The pond provides a place for solitude.

opposites. But not for me. Connecting and being disconnected are part of the same phenomenon. I need both, regularly and in near equal amounts. It is not difficult to find opportunities to be with others—indeed, the invitations to do so come regularly. It is more difficult to find the opportunity to be alone these days, especially in the face of those who do not subscribe to its importance and who see those who seek it as antisocial and strange. And so I travel to Roshara, often alone for several days, in search of solitude.

I am stimulated by others. New ideas fly around the room during a good discussion. I especially appreciated my graduate students at the University of Wisconsin, since our earliest days at Roshara. They bombarded me with fresh ideas, new ways of connecting old thoughts, questions I couldn't answer, perspectives I'd never considered. But after hours of this rich stimulation, I needed to escape, to find a place alone where I could make sense of all that I was taking in—these raw and unexamined ideas and perspectives. So I sought the solitude of my land. I would sit on a hill at the back of the farm and try and make sense out of all that my mind had received.

As I told my students, I am constantly searching for my own truth, my own take on matters, my perspective, my way of understanding the world. I resist the blank acceptance of others' truths as my own, no matter how powerful their reputations, how careful their arguments, or how passionate their pleas. But I listen carefully to other people's positions, whether they are students or learned scholars (whatever that means). I force myself to consider the perspectives of those who appear to have different views from what I value and believe. My stance is that I cannot know what I believe about something unless I know what I *don't* believe, unless I know the counterargument to my position. Thus, I go looking for unusual perspectives, arguments that on the surface anger or agitate me, beliefs that astound and surprise me. It is the old, tired perspectives, spoken in rote and repeated again and again, that tire me and turn me away, turn me off.

Solitude allows you to discover the you that you may not know exists. It is a way to see bigger pictures and larger connections. In solitude we can think through problems slowly and deliberately, searching for and considering multiple perspectives and alternative solutions.

My farm is a place for solitude, where I can sit on the edge of my prairie at sunset on a warm summer evening with a cool southwest breeze washing over me, or walk the trail through the woods on a cool day in autumn when the aspen are deep yellow and the maples bright red. Snowshoe to the pond on a winter day when fresh snow gathers on my coat and

Winter is a quiet, restful time at the farm.

I can see but a few feet in front of me because the snow is falling so fast. Watch raindrops strike the smooth surface of the pond, each little whirlpool becoming ever larger and disappearing, only to be replaced again and again by other raindrops.

Like me, Ruth craves solitude. Her favorite place is on top of the hill, near the white pine windbreak, where she can see across the expanse of our prairie. There a soft breeze rustles the pine needles, the horizon is far in the distance, and the subtle smells of the outdoors surround her. A bench is tucked under a pine tree—Ruth's bench. This is her spot for solitude.

Over the years, I have introduced my children and grandchildren to solitude and its values—not an easy thing to teach, if indeed it can be taught at all. Solitude is personal, to be discovered, and Roshara is a place to do it.

Chapter 27

Roshara Sounds

"The silence was beyond the ordinary sounds of nature; it dealt with distance, timelessness, and a perception, a sense of being engulfed by something greater where minor sounds were only a part, a hush embedded in our consciousness."

SIGURD OLSON

A pair of sandhill cranes nests at the pond each year. Their prehistoric call is distinctive.

Snow-covered
trees hang low over
a farm trail.

Some people love the noice of the city, say it makes them feel alive, gives them a sense of oneness with a vibrant place. But not this country boy. I seek the quiet of the country. Many of my city friends have grown up in the city, love it, respect it, and could not live anywhere else. Most of them are uneasy when there are moments of utter quiet, when there is a break in a radio program or when the TV screen goes blank for a few seconds. They'll switch stations, not content to have a few moments of silence within the blare of continuous programming.

The country is not entirely a quiet place. But there are moments when there is little or no sound. Of course, the ideal country place has no background traffic noise, but those places are becoming more difficult to find as highways and automobiles are sneaking into the far corners of the countryside, invading the quiet and destroying remoteness.

The sounds of the country change with the seasons, especially here in the Midwest, where seasonal change is often dramatic. The sounds of winter are the northwest wind sifting across my prairie, picking up wisps of snow and dropping it again in intricate patterns, rills and ridges, swirls and squiggles. On a cold night in January, the sound of winter is the wind tearing at the cabin, trying to seep in around the windows and doors, challenging my woodstoves, and making a most mournful sound in the process.

Winter sounds can also be the most subtle. On a still day in November, when the temperature is just below freezing and the first heavy snow of the season arrives, the snowflakes, some of them huge, fall ever so lightly on naked tree limbs and dead prairie grass.

An unexpected sound is that of tree fibers exploding on below-zero days. I remember walking in our oak woods one quiet January morning, when the temperature was ten below zero. The only sound was the occasional crow calling in the distance, until I heard what I was sure was a rifle shot. I learned later from my father that it was tree fibers loudly protesting the cold. The sound happens infrequently enough to surprise the cold-weather walker in the woods each time he or she hears it.

The most mysterious of winter sounds might be the northwest wind shaking the dead leaves of the black oaks that still hang on the branches. Some have called this sound a death rattle—and in a way it is. The oak leaves hang on until spring and then finally fall off to make way for new growth and the summer sound of warm breezes moving through green leaves.

Country people wait for the most joyous sound of all, especially if the winter has been long and cold. It comes usually in March, when the wind swings around to the south and the temperature creeps above freezing for a few days. Meltwater begins dripping from the cabin roof and running in rivulets down the trail leading to the white pine woods. It is a sound of celebration. A time for stopping work and listening to the first hints of spring. A time to begin looking forward with anticipation instead of marking time as winter days seem to go on forever.

Soon the sounds of spring fill the air at Roshara, with the first robin song, sometimes when snow piles still line the driveway. The call of Canada geese rings out, the birds flying in formation from their wintering grounds in southern Illinois to the northern reaches of Canada. On an early spring morning it is not uncommon to hear male turkeys gobbling deep in the woods west of our pond. A ruffed grouse's drumming, a crow cawing, or an owl hooting will set them off, prompting a gobbler to let loose with a loud, "gobble, gobble, gobble." And not to be forgotten, sandhill cranes that nest at the pond sound that primitive, rattling call.

When the spring peepers begin their evening chant, I know for sure spring is here. These tiny frogs who live near the pond sing in unison—hundreds of them, perhaps thousands. On a warm, still night their sound engulfs the valley around the pond.

Slowly, imperceptibly, the sounds of summer emerge: the rumble of distant thunder, the deep "jug of rum, more rum" call of the bullfrogs at the pond, the loud snort of a deer when she first discovers me, the dry sound of an August wind moving over the parched prairie, the nervous quivering of aspen leaves, the chatting of a wren outside our bedroom window, and, on occasional hot nights, the sawing of cicadas.

And then the crickets take over the night, and I know it's fall. Occasionally we hear a coyote yapping or an owl calling. And in the morning there is the crunching sound when I walk on frost-covered grass to fetch an armload of wood from the woodshed and I catch the sound of a high-flying V of Canada geese. In the cabin I soon hear the snap and pop of pine kindling wood as the fire in the woodstove comes to life once more.

At the edge of the prairie, a solitary bluebird house awaits the arrival of its first spring occupant.

Chapter 28

◇◇◇◇◇◇◇◇◇◇◇◇◇◇◇◇◇◇

Living on the Land

"When one tugs at a single thing in nature, he finds it attached to the rest of the world."
JOHN MUIR

When my father first bought this old farm in 1964, his neighbors wondered why he was buying more land, and at his age (he was sixty-four at the time). He already owned 160 acres, which he had farmed almost his entire life. Why buy a farm that in the minds of most people, especially farmers, was right close to worthless property? The buildings were falling down; the house had burned. The land was sandy, hilly, and in some places stony. Most of its fields hadn't raised a decent crop for years, if ever. The previous owner had rented out a couple of less hilly fields to a neighbor for corn. But unless it rained every week during the summer—which seldom happened—the corn was doomed to a low yield at best and dried-up plants at worst.

"Don't really know why I bought the place," Dad said to his neighbors, who shook their heads, wondering if Dad had slipped a cog or two as he'd gotten older. But Dad knew what he was doing; he just didn't think his neighbors would understand if he tried to explain it. Besides being a farmer, Dad was keenly interested in wildlife, trees, wildflowers, and birds. He enjoyed sunrises and sunsets, snowstorms and thunder, first snow and the coming of spring. He liked the smell of freshly turned soil and dead grass in August, the sounds of the country night—whip-poor-wills, hoot owls, and crickets. And he loved the seasonal changes, looking forward to each with great anticipation—spring's plowing and planting, summer's harvests, fall's leaves turning color, and winter's slowing down and opportunities to go ice fishing.

Dad was captivated by the land and its multiple meanings and uses. Although I never heard him say it, land was important to him, and his relationship to it was deep and enduring.

The United States does not have an especially good record of how its residents have treated the land. Upon meeting the Native Americans who had fished, hunted, and cultivated the country for thousands of years, the first settlers couldn't understand the Native American philosophy expressed in such phrases as, "The land is sacred," "We and the land are one," "Mother Earth."

The first thing white settlers wanted was to own land. Some early pioneers in central Wisconsin bought newly surveyed land for as little as $1.25 an acre and set out to eke out a living for their families by growing a few crops and raising a few hogs and a couple cows. They were subsistence farmers. For these early settlers, cheap land meant a chance to improve their lives. Many of these early landowners quickly learned that never-before-plowed land would grow spectacular crops of wheat. Soon this former Indian country had been transformed into thousands of acres of wheat. The land view had moved from the sacred to the mundane— from something to be revered to a commercial opportunity.

By the late 1860s wheat growing dwindled, yields plummeted, insects and disease took their toll, and farmers slowly shifted from wheat to dairy farming. Land use changed again. Farmers had learned to rotate their crops: oats, hay crops, pasture, and corn. Cow manure spread back on the fields provided fertilizer, and wheat-worn fields slowly improved.

By the 1950s, with mechanization including milking machines, tractors, field combines, and forage harvesters, dairy farms began increasing in size, as did dairy herds. A farm of 160 acres was no longer large enough to support sufficient cows to be competitive. So farms got bigger, dairy herds grew larger, and farmers with smaller acreages or those with poorer soils were forced to sell.

On the poorer, hillier farms of central Wisconsin, yet another shift in land use unfolded. Former small dairy farms became private hunting preserves, the land essentially allowed to go back to trees. Other little farms met a different fate: they were chopped up into smaller pieces and sold for home building. At the 160-acre farm where I grew up, a home now stands on each of four twenty-acre fields—some modest manufactured homes, one a huge trophy house. Forty acres are devoted to Christmas tree growing. On the remaining forty stand the original homestead buildings—house, barn, granary, pump house—an original oak woodlot, and another new home on a few acres.

I believe it is important that some parcels of land remain whole. Many wild creatures, including owls, bears, pileated woodpeckers, and even songbirds such as scarlet tanagers, prefer larger areas to live, away from close proximity with humans. For those of us who seek out areas of quiet, larger tracts of land offer sound buffers from traffic noise. And from an aesthetic perspective, nothing is more pleasing to me than looking out over a vast tract of land to the north of my farm. Roshara sits within an area of about seven hundred acres of mostly wooded land—four little lakes and my prairie are the exceptions—that is together in one piece as it has always been, with no road cutting through it. Several people own these acres, but for a variety of reasons they have chosen to leave them as they have always been. Many of these acres have never been farmed, in particular those that surround the lakes. In 2001, as he semiretired, my brother Donald and his wife, Marcie, built a permanent home on his portion of the farm, just to the south of our property. My father would have been pleased to have a permanent resident on the farm, looking out for it as well as enjoying it.

My personal views about land, developed from my growing-up years on a farm and from my forty-plus years caring for Roshara, include a strong belief that land is something to cherish and revere, to pass on to those who follow in better condition than when it was acquired. Our farm is a source of fresh vegetables for eating, trails for hiking, paths for skiing and snowshoeing, hills for sunset watching, fields for running, wildflowers to appreciate, and birds and animals to study. It is a storehouse of history and stories.

My land is also a guide and a listener. When I face some crisis in my life—the loss of a loved one, a professional disappointment, a health challenge—I sit on a hill surrounded by sky and acres of trees and grass. This helps me heal.

My farm is always changing, but forever the same. I know a good deal about this old place, but there remains much more to learn. I try to follow what others have taught me: to listen, watch, experience, study, dig into history, look for old barbwire, search out a gully, watch a hawk soar on a cloudless day—and never forget to take care of the land.

Appendix

Every piece of land has a story to tell. The more I learned about my farm, the more stories emerged—and the more digging I wanted to do. I had learned something about the farm from the neighbors who had passed on stories from generation to generation as a part of the oral history of the place: stories of Indians who camped at our pond and visited the homestead bartering maple sugar for salt; tales about the farming strategies of the Coombes family, who owned our farm before we did. (It seemed all the neighbors had stories about Weston Coombes and his mother, Ina, and their trips around the area with horse and buggy during the years when everyone else drove a car.)

After we bought the place, neighbors were quick to point out that it "wasn't much of a farm." They were referring to the hilly and rocky land and the sandy soil. The more I heard, the more questions I had. Why was the region so sandy, hilly, and studded with stones? And what about the Indians who had camped on the pond—who were they, why were they traveling across what later became our land? Could I learn more about the Coombes family, something of their background and their history? It seemed the more I learned about the place, the more remained to be discovered. Over the past forty years I've learned a considerable amount about the farm, but more stories lurk on these acres.

For those who want to learn more about a particular piece of land, here are a few tips. Most of the digging for information can be a bit tedious, with a fair share of dead ends and disappointment, but, oh, what joy it is to uncover a kernel of new knowledge. Perhaps the most fruitful bit of information I uncovered in my search was first landowner Tom Stewart's Civil War records. With those records, I now had a copy of his marriage license, a list of his children, his medical records—I learned more about Tom Stewart than about almost anyone I know.

Some of the best places to look for information are city and town halls, county courthouses, local historical societies, local libraries, cemeteries, and knowledgeable people in the community. The Wisconsin Historical Society in Madison is a wonderful source of all kinds of information,

The pond reflects the vivid fall colors of maples and aspen.

from census and cemetery records to photographs and maps to a vast collection of newspapers; the Society's Web site (wisconsinhistory.org) is an equally diverse and massive source of facts and assistance. The Wisconsin Historical Society, in conjunction with the University of Wisconsin System and the Superior (Wisconsin) Public Library, also shares many of its collections via a network of Area Research Centers at UW campus libraries throughout the state (to find an ARC near you, visit wisconsinhistory.org/libraryarchives/arcnet).

Here are some approaches and sources I used in digging out information about my old farm.

Legal Land Description. To get started tracking down information about a specific piece of land, look at a property tax bill for the legal description; it usually includes county, township (a number), and range (a number). This information from the original land survey tells exactly where the land is located. If you don't own the land you're researching, you can ask the landowner for the legal description or obtain the legal description from the register of deeds at the courthouse in the county where the land is located.

Wisconsin Public Land Survey. With the legal land description in hand, you can find the land's original survey notes. The Wisconsin Historical Society Archives has a microfilm version of the complete surveyors' field notes, made between 1830 and 1866, for every section in each township in Wisconsin. Surveyors described in detail the local vegetation, land features, and evidence of human habitation. You can view these survey notes on microfilm at the Wisconsin Historical Society headquarters building in Madison, reserve them at any of the Area Research Centers, or request them via interlibrary loan. The surveyors' field notes are Archives Series 701. (For more about Wisconsin's first land surveys, see page 23.)

Abstract of Title. This document lists everyone who has owned a piece of land. A new owner usually receives an abstract of title with the purchase documents; land ownership records are also available at the county's register of deeds office.

Plat Books. These county maps that show owners township by township are produced irregularly. Some counties print them every year; others skip a year or more at a time. You can usually find these at local historical societies.

Land Patents Database. The U.S. Bureau of Land Management (BLM) maintains records of all federal land patents (transfers of land from the federal government to individuals). A database of these records, searchable by patentee name, is available online at www.glorecords.blm.gov; researchers can also request certified copies of land patents from the BLM by mail using an online form.

Roster of Wisconsin Volunteers: War of the Rebellion, 1861–1865. This is a complete list of all the Wisconsin men who fought in the Civil War, including their rank and unit. The printed two-volume set is available at many libraries, including the Wisconsin Historical Society Library in Madison, and a searchable digital version is available online at wisconsinhistory.org/roster.

U.S. National Archives and Records Administration. The NARA maintains service and pension records for those who fought in United States wars. Researchers can view the original records at the National Archives in Washington, DC, or use National Archives Trust Fund Form 85 (pension information) or Form 85 (service records) to request the information. To obtain a copy of Form 85 or Form 86, e-mail inquire@nara.gov, or write the U.S. National Archives and Records Administration, 700 Pennsylvania Avenue NW, Washington, DC 20408–0002.

State of Wisconsin Census Reports. Census reports list the names of land occupants by county and township. The census is done every ten years and closed to researchers for seventy-two years. Census data can be accessed on microfilm at the Wisconsin Historical Society or via interlibrary loan (be sure to ask for the Wisconsin reels). There are many reels for each decade, so unless you know where and when a person lived, searching the census material can be a near-impossible task. When I looked at census material for Tom Stewart, I guessed (correctly) that he had not left Waushara County after he sold this land. I found him in the census reports of a nearby township. I also knew when he sold the farm, so I began searching the census records for the year closest to the time he left Rose Township.

Cemetery Records. Many counties have cemetery records online, providing much useful information, including birth and death dates. Cemetery records are available from cemetery associations and from local churches. Sometimes, when I know someone has belonged to a particular church, I go to that church's cemetery and check tombstones—a time-consuming task for a large cemetery. But many cemeteries are quite small. I often pick up additional information about the residents of a community from these cemetery searches.

Local Newspapers. I spend hours searching through old newspapers to learn about a specific community at a given time. For instance, Patterson Memorial Library in Wild Rose has a collection of *The Wild Rose Times*. In those newspapers I read stories about Wild Rose, its businesses, the prices of items for sale, how often the train ran, and of course the local gossip about who visited whom. Not to be overlooked are the obituaries, where I confirm information I've found in cemetery and other records. The Wisconsin Historical Society has available on microfilm a nearly complete collection of every newspaper published in Wisconsin.

FOR MORE ON EARLY LAND RESIDENTS

Kessing, Felix M. *The Menomini Indians of Wisconsin*. Madison: University of Wisconsin Press, 1987. Detailed treaty information, early history to modern-day activities.

Satz, Ronald N. *Chippewa Treaty Rights*. Madison: Wisconsin Academy of Sciences, Arts and Letters, 1991. Information on early Chippewa treaties and more.

Smith, Alice E. *The History of Wisconsin*. Vol. I, *From Exploration to Statehood*. Madison: State Historical Society of Wisconsin, 1973.

Wisconsin Cartographers Guild. *Wisconsin's Past and Present: A Historical Atlas*. Madison: University of Wisconsin Press, 1998. Information about early cultures in the state, immigrants, and much more.

Wyman, Mark. *The Wisconsin Frontier*. Bloomington: Indiana University Press, 1998.

Zaniewski, Kazimierz, and Carol J. Rosen. *The Atlas of Ethnic Diversity in Wisconsin*. Madison: University of Wisconsin Press, 1998. Includes information about Native American tribe locations as well as where various ethnic groups settled in the state.

FOR MORE ON THE LAND

Martin, Lawrence. *The Physical Geography of Wisconsin*. Madison: University of Wisconsin Press, 1965. Information about the glaciers, land formation, and much more.

Wisconsin Geological and Natural History Survey, Madison. This agency has maps of soil types for most counties in the state.

FOR MORE ON AGRICULTURAL CROPS

Current, Richard. *The History of Wisconsin*. Vol. II, *The Civil War Era 1848–1873*. Madison: State Historical Society of Wisconsin, 1976.

Schafer, Joseph. *A History of Agriculture in Wisconsin*. Madison: State Historical Society of Wisconsin, 1922. An excellent reference for the early history of farming in Wisconsin, including extensive coverage of the wheat-growing years.

United States Department of Agriculture, National Agricultural Statistics Service, Wisconsin. Provides agricultural statistics, county by county—crop yields, numbers of livestock, etc.

FOR MORE ON IDENTIFYING PLANTS AND ANIMALS

GENERAL

Bates, John. *Trailside Botany*. Duluth, MN: Pfeifer-Hamilton, 1995.

Edsall, Marian S. *Roadside Plants and Flowers: A Traveler's Guide to the Midwest and Great Lakes Area*. Madison: University of Wisconsin Press, 1985.

Hoffman, Randy. *Wisconsin's Natural Communities*. Madison: University of Wisconsin Press, 2002.

WILDFLOWERS AND GRASSES

Courtenay, Booth, and James Zimmerman. *Wild Flowers and Weeds*. New York: Van Nostrand Reinhold Company, 1972.

Curtis, John T. *The Vegetation of Wisconsin*. Madison: University of Wisconsin Press, 1959, 1971. Explains the biological tension zone and offers descriptions of Wisconsin's varied plant communities.

Ladd, David. *Tallgrass Prairie Wild Flowers: A Field Guide*. Guilford, CT: Falcon, 1995.

Tekiela, Stan. *Wildflowers of Wisconsin*. Cambridge, MN: Adventure Publications, 2000.

Wells, Diana. *100 Flowers and How They Got Their Names*. Chapel Hill, NC: Algonquin Books, 1997.

BIRDS

Bull, John, and John Farrand Jr. *The Audubon Society Field Guide to North American Birds: Eastern Region*. New York: Alfred A. Knopf, 1977.

Gromme, Owen J. *Birds of Wisconsin*. Revised ed. Madison: University of Wisconsin Press, 1998.

Sibley, David Allen. *The Sibley Guide to Birds*. New York: Alfred A. Knopf, 2000.

Tekiela, Stan. *Birds of Wisconsin*. Cambridge, MN: Adventure Publications, 1999.

TREES

Little, Elbert L. *National Audubon Society Field Guide to North American Tress: Eastern Region*. New York: Alfred A. Knopf, 1980.

Petrides, George A. *A Field Guide to Trees and Shrubs*. Peterson Field Guide Series. Boston: Houghton Mifflin, 1972.

For information about Wisconsin's Forestry Stewardship Program, contact the Wisconsin Department of Natural Resources.

ANIMALS

Reid, Fiona. *Peterson Field Guide to Mammals of North America*. 4th ed. Boston: Houghton Mifflin, 2006.

FOR BACKGROUND AND INSPIRATION

Carson, Rachel. *Silent Spring*. Boston: Houghton Mifflin Company, 1962.

Christofferson, Bill. *The Man from Clear Lake: Earth Day Founder Gaylord Nelson*. Madison: University of Wisconsin Press, 2004.

Emerson, Ralph Waldo. *The Selected Writings of Ralph Waldo Emerson*. New York: The Modern Library, 1992.

Leopold, Aldo. *A Sand County Almanac*. New York: Oxford University Press, 1949.

Muir, John. *The Story of My Boyhood and Youth*. Madison: University of Wisconsin Press, 1965.

Olson, Sigurd F. *Listening Point*. Minneapolis: University of Minnesota Press, 1997.

Thoreau, Henry David. *Walden*. New York: W. W. Norton, 1951.

Notes

CHAPTER 3

1. Lawrence Martin, *The Physical Geography of Wisconsin* (Madison: University of Wisconsin Press, 1965), 235–270.

2. A. R. Whitson, W. J. Geib, G. Conroy, A. K. Kuhlman, and J. W. Nelson, *Soil Survey of Waushara County* (Madison: Wisconsin Geological and Natural History Survey, 1913).

3. Augustine J. Otter, Fred J. Simeth, and Duane T. Simonson, *Soil Survey of Waushara Country, Wisconsin* (Madison: USDA Soil Conservation Service and College of Agricultural and Life Sciences, University of Wisconsin–Madison, 1989).

4. Ibid., 34.

5. Ibid., 20.

6. A. R. Whitson, W. J. Geib, G. Conroy, A. K. Kuhlman, and J. W. Nelson. *Soil Survey of Waushara County* (Madison: Wisconsin Geological and Natural History Survey, 1913).

7. United States Department of Agriculture, National Agricultural Statistics Service, Wisconsin-Waushara County, 2006.

8. John T. Curtis, *The Vegetation of Wisconsin* (Madison: University of Wisconsin Press, 1959, 1971), 15–24.

9. Lawrence Martin, *The Physical Geography of Wisconsin* (Madison: University of Wisconsin Press, 1965), 254–255.

CHAPTER 4

1. "Exterior Field Notes T21N R9E R10E," May 9, 1851, *Wisconsin Public Land Survey Records: Original Field Notes and Plat Maps.*

2. Ibid., 53.

3. "Interior Field Notes," October 2, 1851, *Wisconsin Public Land Survey Records: Original Field Notes and Plat Maps*, 300.

4. Ibid., 345.

5. Ibid.

6. Felix Keesing, *The Menomini Indians of Wisconsin: A Study of Three Centuries of Cultural Contact and Change* (Madison: University of Wisconsin Press, 1987), 140–147.

7. Ibid., 139.

8. Ibid., 141.

9. Ibid., 142.

10. *Wisconsin Public Land Survey Records: Original Field Notes and Plat Maps.*

11. "Interior Field Notes," October 2, 1851, *Wisconsin Public Land Survey Records: Original Field Notes and Plat Maps*, 319.

12. Bureau of Land Management, *Wisconsin Land Patents Database: Waushara County*, Washington, DC: National Archives.

13. Ibid.

CHAPTER 5

1. John M. Woodward, unpublished manuscript, c. 1925, Wild Rose Historical Society, Wild Rose, WI.

2. Ibid.

3. Ibid.

CHAPTER 6

1. Roster Wisconsin Volunteers, 35th Infantry, Company 5, 566.

2. William Striedy, Affidavit to Origin of Disability, May June, 1897, U.S. National Archives and Records Administration, Full Pension File, Thomas Stewart.

3. James Gustins, Affidavit for Commissioned Officer or Comrade, no date, U.S. National Archives and Records Administration, Full Pension File, Thomas Stewart.

4. War Department, Adjutant General's Office, October 30, 1882, U.S. National Archives and Records Administration, Full Pension File, Thomas Stewart.

5. Abstract of Title, Lands in Section 33-20-10. Waushara Abstract Corporation, Wautoma, WI. Abstract Number 215, 1.

6. Richard Current, *The History of Wisconsin*. Vol. II, *The Civil War Era 1848–1873* (Madison: State Historical Society of Wisconsin, 1976), 94.

7. Ibid., 92.

8. Certificate of Marriage, Tom Stewart and Maria Jenks, August 28, 1869, Register of Deeds, Waushara County, Wautoma, WI.

9. Bureau of Land Management, *Wisconsin Land Patents Database: Waushara County*, Washington, DC: National Archives.

10. State of Wisconsin Census, Town of Rose, Waushara County, June 1875.

11. The *Waushara Argus* (Wautoma, WI), June 9, 1875.

12. John M. Woodward, unpublished manuscript, c. 1925, Wild Rose Historical Society, Wild Rose, WI.

13. "Wild Rose History, Stories by Members," unpublished manuscript, no date, Patterson Memorial Library, Wild Rose, WI.

14. Cemetery Records, Mt. Pleasant Cemetery (Standalone Cemetery), Waushara County, WI.

CHAPTER 7

1. Waushara Abstract Corporation, Wautoma, WI, Abstract of Title, Lands in Section 33-20-10, Abstract Number 215, 1–15.

2. *Portrait and Biographical Album of Green Lake, Marquette and Waushara Counties, Wisconsin* (Chicago: Acme Publishing Company, 1890).

3. Minutes of Village Board, Wild Rose, WI, C. A. Smart, President, April 25, 1904.

4. Notice, *Wild Rose Times* (Wild Rose, WI), March 19, 1905.

5. Waushara Abstract Corporation, Wautoma, WI, Abstract of Title, Lands in Section 33-20-10, Abstract Number 215, 1–15.

6. Minutes of Village Board, Wild Rose, WI, August 1, 1908.

7. *Wild Rose Times* (Wild Rose, WI), February 15, 1912.

8. *Atlas and Farmers' Directory, Rose Township* (St. Paul, MN: The Farmer, circa 1913), 11.

9. Ibid.

10. Ibid.

CHAPTER 15

1. Virgil J. Vogel. *Indian Names on Wisconsin's Map* (Madison: University of Wisconsin Press, 1991), 64.

CHAPTER 16

1. Rob Nurre, personal correspondence, September 5, 2006.

CHAPTER 18

1. Diana Wells, *100 Flowers and How They Got Their Names* (Chapel Hill, NC: Algonquin Books, 1997), 62–63.

2. Ibid., 121–122.

Index

Page numbers in **bold** indicate illustrations.

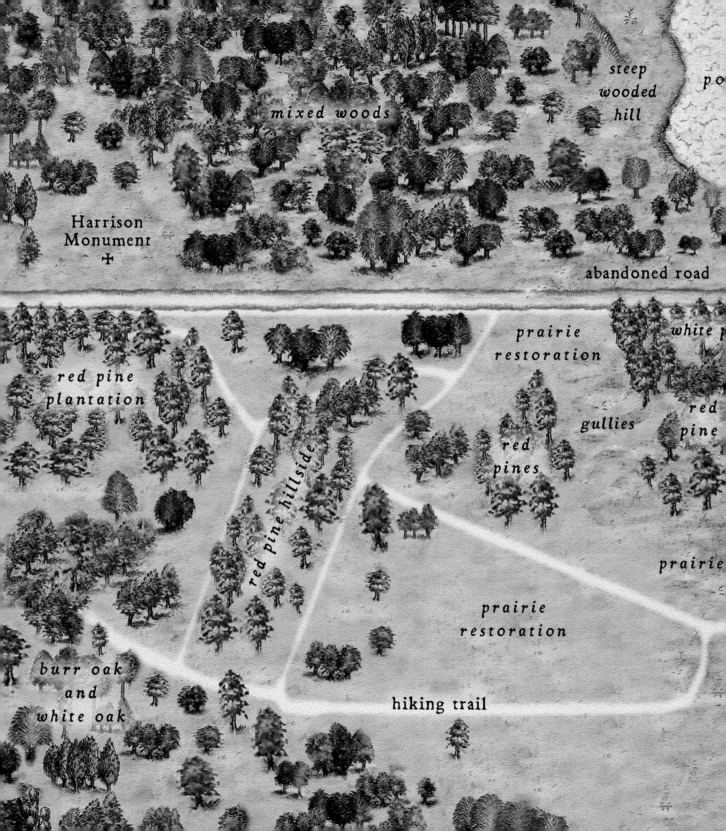